THE FORGOTTEN SERVICE

Also available in this series:

Peter Austen	THE COUNTRY ANTIQUE DEALER
John Bailey	TALES OF THE COUNTRY ESTATES
Mary Barnard	DIARY OF AN OPTIMIST
Pip Beck	A WAAF IN BOMBER COMMAND
Adrian Bell	THE CHERRY TREE
Mary Sydney Burke	THE SOLDIER'S WIFE
Jennifer Davies	TALES OF THE OLD GYPSIES
Kathleen Dayus	THE GHOSTS OF YESTERYEAR
Richard van Emden	VETERANS: THE LAST SURVIVORS OF
and Steve Humphries	THE GREAT WAR
Jean Faley	UP OOR CLOSE
Ken Hankins	A CHILD OF THE THIRTIES
Herbert C. Harrison	THE MILL HOUSE AND
	THEREABOUTS
Gregory Holyoake	THE PREFAB KID
Erma Harvey James	WITH MAGIC IN MY EYES
Joy Lakeman	THEM DAYS
Brian P. Martin	TALES FROM THE COUNTRY PUB
	TALES OF THE OLD COUNTRYWOMEN
Roger Mason	GRANNY'S VILLAGE
Katherine Moore	QUEEN VICTORIA IS VERY ILL
J. C. Morten	I REMAIN, YOUR SON JACK
and Sheila Morten	
Pauline Neville	PEGGY
Humphrey Phelps	UNCLE GEORGE AND COMPANY
Tom Quinn	TALES OF THE OLD COUNTRY
	FARMERS
Edward Storey	LETTERS FROM THE FENS
Elizabeth West	HOVEL IN THE HILLS
William Woodrow	ANOTHER TIME, ANOTHER PLACE

THE FORGOTTEN SERVICE

AUXILIARY AMBULANCE
STATION 39
WEYMOUTH MEWS

Angela Raby

While looking through this book you'll say
"Their days are spent in leisure",
No doubt to you, it looks that way,
To us, it's not all pleasure.

Babette Loraine
Station 39
February 1940

ISIS
LARGE PRINT
Oxford and Orlando

First published in Great Britain 1999
by After the Battle

Published in Large Print 2000 by ISIS Publishing Ltd,
7 Centremead, Osney Mead, Oxford OX2 0ES, and
ISIS Publishing, PO Box 195758,
Winter Springs, Florida 32719-5758, USA
by arrangement with Angela Raby

British Library Cataloguing in Publication Data
Raby, Angela
    The forgotten service : Auxiliary Ambulance Station 39. –
    Large print ed.
    1. Raby, Angela 2. Ambulance service – Great Britain 3. Large
    type books
    I. Title
    362.1'88'0941

ISBN 0-7531-5799-3 (hb)
ISBN 0-7531-9600-X (pb)

Printed and bound by Antony Rowe, Chippenham and Reading

AUTHOR'S ACKNOWLEDGEMENT

May Greenup, my aunt, died at the age of ninety-five. She was blind in her latter years yet she devoted uncountable hours enthusiastically discussing her role of Station Officer in the London Auxiliary Ambulance Service. She provided a wealth of photographs, drawings, documents and official records. May was the motive force behind this book and I dedicate it to her.

I owe much to Babette Loraine who served with May. Her personal memories of Station 39 and the photographs and documents she provided were invaluable.

Terry Spurr, M.B.E. the curator of the London Ambulance Service NHS Trust Museum at Ilford gave extensive help with the provision of documentation and photographs for which I am extremely grateful.

I also extend my thanks to all those who have provided interesting and informative material, particularly Stephanie Currie who served at Watford Station.

Anyone who is not initiated early in life to the mysteries of the computer could face a frustrating battle. I succeeded due to the patience and skills of Christina and Tim, who were often on the other end of a telephone. Moreover Tim provided all the hardware, maintaining and updating as appropriate.

My love to Leo, who not only gave vital support and imaginative advice throughout the project but also restored my confidence in my creative abilities.

Angela Raby

CONTENTS

Foreword 1X

Introduction X1

1. Frances May Tuckwell 1

2. First Impressions 12

3. Weymouth Mews 42

4. Action Stations 67

5. Incident 707 129

6. Personalities 148

7. Victory Celebrations 176

8. Postscript 187

FOREWORD

ROSEMARY DAY
Chairman London Ambulance Service 1995-1999

Before television serials such as *Casualty* and documentaries like *Front Line*, the Ambulance Service remained to most people the forgotten "front line" of the Health Service. Managed until the 1950s as part of local government, it was only after transfer to the NHS that it was recognised as a vital service which could make the difference between life and death for serious accident victims; between recovery to a good quality of life or not, and between courage and despair for many elderly patients.

This book, of personal reminiscence, unique records, illustrations and drawings of a life under fire that we today can hardly imagine, does for the wartime London Auxiliary Ambulance Service what television has done for the Service of today.

The Forgotten Service has been thoughtfully and lovingly put together. It gives a picture for the first time of the thousands of people, from a huge variety of backgrounds, who worked for very little pay and almost no recognition doing a tough and difficult job. The courage of the L.A.A.S. in reaching and helping civilians injured in the great London raids of 1940-41 and then again with the "doodlebugs" and rockets of 1944 and 1945 is only matched by the appalling task they had to undertake to recover the dead. *The Forgotten*

Service illustrates in the documents, poems and photographs what daily life and work was like. It also shows how much depended not on technology but on each individual knowing and then doing the job.

It is extraordinary that while there is so much material produced about the 1939-1945 war, the Auxiliary Ambulance Service has still largely been forgotten. Angela Raby's book fills this gap superbly. I am sure that all who read it will, like me, marvel at the spirit and bravery of so many "ordinary" people to help their fellow men at time of desperate need, and will always remember the images captured so vividly in the drawings and photographs.

INTRODUCTION

The contribution that the Ambulance Service made towards the war effort has been virtually ignored. When searching for written or visual records, this deficiency becomes apparent. There appears to have been no significant media coverage of the service, no fiction or non-fiction films or books or television programmes relating to it; no museum records or tableaux and no active members of the service have recorded their experiences.

For example, the comprehensive section on the war at York's Castle Museum boasts only one Ambulance Service issue helmet without comment attached to this isolated item. Police, A.R.P, Nurses, Home Guard, Fire Services and the Land Army are covered by tableaux, written records and photographs. This dearth of recognition in general collections is echoed nationwide. In this context to find no mention of the dozens of Auxiliary Ambulance Stations commissioned in London during the war should elicit no surprise. All records are thought to have been destroyed at the end of hostilities for the estimated 10,000 auxiliaries. Although the London Ambulance Service NHS Trust Museum at Ilford has unique displays covering ambulance services in general from 1880, the Curator had no records of auxiliaries until fortunately six record files of volunteers dating from 1939 were unearthed in 1998.

Maybe the reason for the lack of interest in the Service stems from the difficulties the usual media glamorisation would have presented. One has only to look at *Dad's Army* or more recently *The Land Girls* to appreciate the format. It is difficult fifty years on to comprehend fully the gruesome content of their work, given the current experiences of a modern ambulance service. Not only responding to emergencies through air raids but collecting casualties with appalling injuries was doubly awful when these were civilians. A description of the collection of dismembered bodies, often rat-eaten, elicited a casual remark that people would not believe how heavy a severed leg was to lift, especially after working all day on a factory floor. Transporting these assorted bits and pieces of bodies to the largest refrigeration system in London, turned one ambulance driver against fish for years. Nevertheless humour was the catalyst that kept these crews cemented together, and obliterated, at least for a while, the horror.

Asking for information about wartime service is regularly to elicit dead silence. Those who had daily been witnessing horrors cannot bring themselves to relive the trauma. (There was no counselling or management of trauma victims in 1940.) Steven Spielberg, giving an interview on the World Service after the launch of his film, *Saving Private Ryan*, explained how his father, having flown in only one combat mission, had been unable to speak to him of the horrors. Spielberg's father, barbecuing some chicken one day, suddenly poured out the story of how he had to collect the remains of his colleagues from their burnt-out plane. Hardened veterans had buried their experiences and never talked even to their families until the dramatic war scenes in the film released the spring causing delayed trauma to many veterans.

Motivation to redress this neglect of the Ambulance Service and specifically the London Auxiliary Ambulance Service from 1939 to 1945 was triggered by conversations and letters from the writer's aunt, May Greenup, who was a volunteer serving during this period at London Auxiliary Ambulance Station 39, St Marylebone, situated in the West End of London. Having joined the service early in the war, May was soon to be promoted to Station Officer.

May Greenup, having gone blind in her eighties, wrote down her memories and showed me unique ambulance memorabilia including her personal administrative standing orders for the running of Station 39 typed on Government 'flimsy'. She also had dozens of photographs of Station 39 personnel as well as senior staff from other stations, her colleagues' illustrations, poems and letters, her certificates and congratulatory letters, and an illustrated diary dated 1941 together with her watercolours of the Station: a forerunner of her subsequent artistic career. This I have placed within the context of her life history by the addition of photographs and letters covering her 95 years.

During sleepless nights she would reminisce over the past to decide on which topic she would write about in the morning. Having sent me the letter, she would follow it up by telephoning to elaborate on details. Throughout the text May's own words have been quoted to give colour whenever appropriate. Her personal reminiscences motivated a general exploration of the Auxiliary Service, incorporating memories recounted by her colleagues and other auxiliaries, together with the procedures garnered from the newly-discovered files. Woven into the account is one, Josephine Butler, whose exploits impinge dramatically on May's report.

This work began as a niece's record of her aunt's reminiscences and expanded into a fascination with a group of wartime volunteers whose experiences were generally as traumatic as any of those who served. These volunteers have been forgotten. They were paid but little and nothing when they were not on duty. With no issued uniform until 1942, they drove old, converted vans and trucks which initially had wooden slats for seats and tarpaulin covers. Cars were an assortment donated freely by civilians. They were awarded few honours, and received no pensions nor post-war gratuities. No one even knows how many were killed or injured. Perhaps before they are all gone, this limited study may help to redress this injustice.

May enjoyed the last joke: I thought I had chosen to become interested in her memories and had offered to organise them. However from an old friend of hers I now understand that May had asked her friend, Elizabeth, how she should preserve her memories and memorabilia: to which Elizabeth had suggested interesting 'one of your nieces'!

A page of May Greenup's reminiscences written when blind with the aid of a writing frame with corrections by her friend Elizabeth Bridge.

CHAPTER ONE

Frances May Tuckwell

May was born on March 4th, 1902 at Water Orton where her father, George Tuckwell, was a Police Constable. Within a few years her father was promoted to Sergeant and the family moved to Lyndon End, Sheldon. Her elder brother, Frank, attended the South Yardley Infants' School but May did not join him because her mother, Mary, preferred to teach her to read, knit and sew at home. A photograph shows May, aged about two, in lacy bonnet, sitting beside Frank wearing his school cap.

When her father was promoted to Inspector of Police at Coleshill in 1909, May attended the Coleshill Church of England Parochial School in Back Lane. Being tall for her age, at seven May was placed in a class with older children. Her cookery exercise book, which she started at the age of twelve, remains from this period. She had written up recipes and essays on cookery practice and kitchen design from 1914 to 1915, and at the end of the book there are some notes on sewing techniques. May remembered how she spent hours practising "gathering, button holes, placket and lace insertion" in the making of a pair of knickers for their final year's garment. On presenting the finished item to Mrs Porter, the Headmistress, she was told that she had put in two right legs. Having been dismissed to undo and remake the garment, in record time May returned to Mrs Porter, the legs adjusted. Unfortunately she had made the same mistake again and was told that if her friend, Grace Clark, had half her dash, and if May had half Grace's thoughtfulness, the result would be an ideal seamstress. The first time she was allowed to use a sewing machine, she promptly speared her finger, causing her to faint. This dash and flair was apparent years later in her oil paintings. She was proficient academically and should have attended a grammar school. However for girls resident in Coleshill there was no comparable school to the boys' grammar school, which her brothers attended. Although Nuneaton and Birmingham possessed grammar schools, her father would not allow her to travel by train.

A photograph taken in 1907 shows her father and eldest brother, Frank, in the front seat of a Calthorpe. On the back seat sits his wife and May, Kathleen and Bernard. May said her father was one of the earliest drivers in the country: he had been test driving cars as early as 1897, much to her mother's concern. He is transporting his family for a month's holiday to Island House, Burford, where grandmother Phoebe lived. While driving on the unmetalled roads May remembers that a labourer temporarily repaired a puncture in a tyre by stuffing in grass. May's father was a friend of the former works manager of the Wolseley Motor Car Company in Drews Lane, Washwood Heath, who left the company to produce the Calthorpe. Being experienced he was invited to test drive and report back with suggested improvements which the mechanics would implement. By 1911 the family consisted of the two girls and four boys, Frank, Bernard, Peter and Victor. May remembers her mother complaining when her patience was sorely tried: "Oh dear, my children make me say things I would never dream of thinking".

At the age of fourteen May became a pupil teacher at Coleshill, studying one day a week at the Marston Green Teacher Centre under the tutelage of Miss E. E. Walker. Later this centre was removed to Castle Bromwich where she pursued her academic studies, taking Oxford Senior Certificate and obtaining three Distinctions in English, History and Geography and Credits in the other subjects. She obtained a place at St Gabriel's College in Camberwell, London, but was unable to attend for two years because she failed the medical due to a thyroid irregularity. During the interim she taught as an uncertificated teacher in schools at Minworth and later Arley. The Headmaster of Minworth, Joseph Greenup (her future father-in-law), wrote that "the enthusiasm of the pupils is a glowing testimony to her methods". The excellent report from Arley states that "she promises to be an exceptionally successful teacher".

In 1922 at the age of twenty she joined the new intake at St Gabriel's College for teacher training at Cormont Road, Camberwell. The Principal was Miss Burns, the renowned former headmistress of Cheltenham Ladies' College. St Gabriel's, established in 1900, was situated in a very lovely building overlooking Myatt's Fields: "a pretty park". The College was totally residential, with over one hundred students in each year. May commented that she did not remember any girl not completing the course even though there were strict rules which May, for one, did not resent. The daily timetable was fixed with a Rising Bell at 7a.m. followed by the Chapel Bell which rang at 7.55a.m for Morning Service which was mandatory for all students. Breakfast followed the service. At 9a.m. study and lectures were attended until 12.45 when the students were dismissed for the lunch served at 1p.m. After lunch, during free time, they were allowed to go out but only if accompanied with a companion. At 3.45p.m. there was an informal tea followed by study until 6p.m. However on Saturday afternoons they were allowed to stay out until 6.30p.m. For dinner in the evenings they were expected to change from the uniform skirt and blazer into a smart frock. At 9p.m. all students attended Evensong and were in bed by 10.15p.m. when the lights would be switched off.

During weekday afternoons May had sufficient time to visit the Tate and the Dulwich Galleries. At the weekends many other galleries, museums, theatres and churches were all within easy distance, instilling in her a lifetime love of this artistic heritage. She also went to the swimming baths and played tennis and hockey during these carefree years. On Sundays they were expected to "worship with the rest of the world" and visited all the well known churches. However May confided that they did not always attend a church service.

On Friday evenings the lecturers held "open room" offering coffee to the students. On Monday morning at

11a.m. there was a rush to the Notice Board in the Common Room to discover who would be "On High" which meant the lucky recipient was chosen to dine at the Principal's table for the next seven days. At dinner each night the chosen student would move round one place to have the opportunity of talking to different staff. Some feared sitting next to the Principal because they became tongue tied: not so May, who remarked that she felt very easy in her presence. All week everything was done for these chosen students: there were no duties, no laundry and no housework. The day before the end of term, the word went round for "Trunks" and the carter, Patterson, collected them and delivered May's to her Warwickshire home for 1/-.

May left in 1924 with a glowing report concluding, "She is a good teacher and disciplinarian". She had found the lecturers excellent and the work easy, attaining Head Student status after the first term. May wrote that she made many friends and really enjoyed the two years knowing that her horizons were enlarged. One might think that the regimentation was oppressive but that discipline stood her in good stead when she was promoted to be in charge of the ambulance station.

Having qualified, May took a teaching post in Tottenham where she lodged with her brother Frank's future brother-in-law. Two years later she married Joseph Greenup, later elected R. I. and A.R.C.A, the son of the Coleshill headmaster. "Jossie" had been awarded a scholarship at the Birmingham School of Art when he was twelve years old. There he met Henry Rushbury and Gerald Brocklehurst. At sixteen he attended the South

Kensington College of Art. He continued his fine art training at the Royal Academy School where he gained several prizes including the Silver Medal for life painting. During the First World War he served as an officer before being seconded into the Flying Corps as an observer.

May and Jossie married in 1926, living at 14 Princes Avenue, Alexandria Park, before moving to Green Lane Studio situated in an artists' colony at Chesham Bois. Jossie was resuming his artistic career by working as an illustrator for newspapers, books and *Pearson's* magazine. Victor, May's youngest brother, remembers Jossie sketching him all dressed up as the Captain Blood to illustrate the novel by Raphael Sabatini.

Elizabeth Bridge, who became May's friend and companion for the next fifty years, was given a letter of introduction to Jossie from the Head of Hornsey School of Art. She worked in Jossie's studio illustrating newspapers and modelling for him: a striking portrait of Elizabeth titled "Distant Horizons" was exhibited at the Coronation Exhibition of Prominent Artists in 1937. She did not follow the family tradition of musicians and composers but was determined to make her living from painting. Around 1930 May started painting in watercolours choosing chiefly landscape subjects. She was elected to the Royal Institute of Water Colourists Club, having several paintings accepted and hung in the annual shows. Aged about four, the author remembers accompanying her on a sketching expedition to Maxstoke Woods where she was given stretched paper on a little board and encouraged to paint in water colours: twelve years later the writer was also at the Birmingham School of Art.

When Jossie began to receive portrait commissions, they moved to 118 Abbey Road, St John's Wood. In 1940 May joined the Auxiliary Ambulance Service as a driver and subsequently was promoted to Station Officer at Weymouth Mews. Her training and natural qualities of leadership were displayed in the difficult times in which she served. For a while her sister, Kathleen, served at the Swiss Cottage Ambulance Station and Elizabeth joined the Fire Service. Jossie continued to tour the country painting portraits of the beautiful and famous, including Princess Elizabeth in Guides' uniform and the King and Queen of Siam. May believed he was involved in secret government activities under the cover of his painting.

After Jossie's death in 1946, May joined forces with Elizabeth and they left London to rent rooms at Charlbury, where Elizabeth, a sensitive and accomplished portrait painter, developed her distinctive and popular style of flower painting from which she made her living. They returned regularly to London to transport paintings to the various galleries. During this period May often visited Yorkshire where her father-in-law was seriously ill. After he died in 1947 May took a teaching post at Oddington near Stow-on-the-Wold. The next year they removed to Redesdale Cottage, a large stonebuilt house set in an imposing position above the village at Bourton-on-the-Hill in the Cotswolds and May retired from teaching to help Elizabeth prepare for her first one-man show at Foyles' London Gallery. A few years later, Elizabeth's card and calendars were chosen by four members of the Royal Family at Christmas.

At this house they had the space to keep a variety of dogs, including German Shepherds, and cats. They utilised the spacious basement for rearing litters of puppies bred from the Shepherds, Mitzie and Biza. Many photographs of their dogs remain frozen by time: they both had a love and devotion to all animals. Hellebores, Christmas Roses and Lenten Lilies filled the garden providing their favourite subjects for painting. May was encouraged by Elizabeth to paint small pictures of flowers, laying on the oil paint with a palette knife. These decorative paintings were most successful, selling in many outlets including Heals and John Lewis of London and in local art galleries in the Cotswolds. However Elizabeth remarked that it was unfair that the critics described these paintings as furnishings. An invoice notes that E. A Robinson of Bristol wishes to keep three paintings which "look very good on the office walls". Tragically all other appreciation and documentation of their artistic careers has been lost.

In 1952 they bought a large cottage-style dwelling, Peewit Cottage at Barton-on-the-Heath. They renovated the house and converted the spacious barn and outhouses into their studios. May started a pottery studio having taken a two-year course at Banbury Art School, selling her work at many outlets. Having nursed both Elizabeth's mother and her sister, Kathleen, in their terminal illnesses, they decided to leave a place so full of sad memories.

In 1968 they bought a derelict and disused school and house, The Old School, at Blaenporth, Cardiganshire. They restored the buildings and converted the canteen into a gallery where Elizabeth's paintings and May's pottery could be displayed for sale. The classrooms became studios for painting and pottery. May noted that often the public would wait to buy pots which were still hot from the kiln, so popular was her work. Living in Wales, the landscape inspired Elizabeth to produce richly subtle watercolours. The series of paintings depicting quarries, in particular, made a powerful statement in contrast with the sensitivity of her floral work. In the seventies she noted that after an illness she ventured into abstraction but soon returned to realism which she preferred.

A reporter, describing in July 1968 the impressive improvements carried out at their studio-home, mentions that knowing they had lived there but a year he was "amazed at the results of their hard work in the garden". May replied that they liked to eat everything fresh. They had been conscious in the fifties for the need to eat a good wholesome diet and to preserve nature. They even refused to allow washing-up detergent to be used in their house. Their love of flowers expressed through their paintings was extended to the vegetable kingdom. The reporter might have added that they had done well considering their ages, May was sixty-six and Elizabeth nine years her junior.

They stayed for seven "good years" but feeling homesick, they returned to the Cotswolds and Broadway in 1973. They bought a house, Briardene, set back behind an orchard on the road to Evesham. Here Elizabeth had a large studio inside the house while May used a pottery in an adjacent building. For nearly twenty years they both worked solidly until May's sight failed in her late eighties. She wrote that both of them had been active creating pictures and pottery and hoped that she might recapture some sight in the future to enable her to work again. Looking back over her life she wrote in 1992: "All this, together with my great interest in Elizabeth's work and career, has made life a wonderfully happy time".

Losing her sight must have been a dreadful affliction for one so seeped in the visual arts and was made more difficult considering her great age. However she never allowed a morsel of self pity to creep into anything she said or wrote.

After Elizabeth's death in December 1996, May realised that she needed to have constant care due to her blindness. She systematically organised the sale of the paintings and contents of Elizabeth's studio, the antique furniture and art books, saying that when the house was emptied she would sell that too and move into a residential home. Deciding what to do with an object, she would hold it in her hand to visualise the book, photo, picture, reminding herself as she listened to the description and then make a decisive decision.

May moved into a residential home in 1997 after selling Briardene. As would be expected from one who so valued ties with the family, she kept in regular touch by telephone. On what was to be the last visit, she offered the author a pile of watercolour sketches she had made during the thirties and forties, remarking they would only be burned when she was gone. Amongst these were found her watercolours of the views around Weymouth Mews, executed while she had a break in the routine. These quickly-executed sketches are immediate and powerful comments, and we see through her eyes the ambulance, the red marker flags and the ephemeral figures clearing snow. They will live on.

After May's death on January 8, 1998, Liz, her niece, found a framed print with the glass broken when she was packing up May's room. An article written by Rev. W. H. Elliott in *The Sunday Graphic* dated July 1949 was folded inside the back of the frame. Liz felt that these words mirrored the feelings experienced on returning from visiting Auntie May.

"Again and again I, who came to cheer and bless, went away ashamed of my own self-pity about little things. It was I who was cheered and blessed."

May scattered Elizabeth's ashes into the source of the Windrush, explaining that the river flowed through the Cotswolds where they had spent so many years and on to London. May's ashes followed.

CHAPTER
TWO

First Impressions

When May Greenup lost her sight in her nineties she gave the author many thousands of photographs that she had taken over the years, including over a hundred of Station 39. Having started to record her memories, the addition of these immediately enriched and illuminated this text. The most poignant of these photos is the portrait of the forlorn stray dog, a black Scottie. He sits isolated in the middle of the Mews, near the Ambulance Station. Symbolically, this dog represents an icon for Station 39's war. These photos show no horrors of their war, only light-hearted snapshots of men and women apparently enjoying themselves. Even an official photo of the wounded returning from Africa shows two soldiers smiling and joking despite their loss of limbs. Although the censor ensured that images which might damage the war effort or create despair amongst the populace were suppressed, there was also a personal censoring to suppress the indescribable horrors enabling duties to be performed. Today it is difficult to engage those who served with the ambulances in reminiscence, and even May narrating gruesome stories made a joke of the horror.

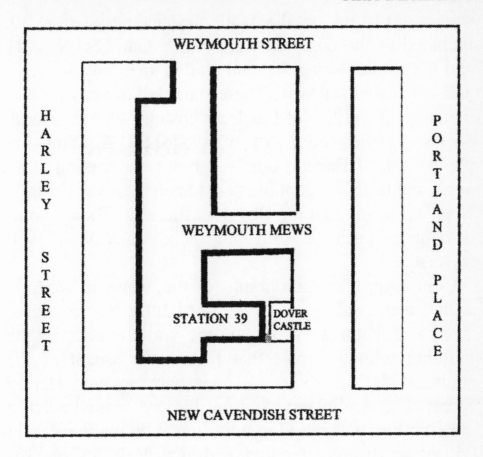

Imagine Weymouth Mews (the site of Station 39) as being like a capital "H" with top extending to Weymouth Street in the north with a base in New Cavendish Street and being sandwiched between Harley Street and Portland Place. The east leg of the "H" is a through road, the Dover Castle Public House being at the south end. The western leg of the Mews has a narrow exit to Weymouth Street at the northern end. The other direction ends in a brick wall: the Scottie dog sits patiently here in the photo. Turning left half-way down this section is a cul-de-sac complete with the garages used by the Auxiliary Ambulance Station. A photo taken by May shows a plaque on the wall announcing Station 39. Included in the complex were Hall's Garages, Nos. 41 and 42: further along this end wall is an archway with a half-concealed stairway. These stairs led directly up into the snug of the Dover Castle, a hostelry on Weymouth Mews — the source of many jokes. An amusing photograph of Babette Loraine shows her leaning at an angle and bears the caption, "Last Seen in Dover Castle!" Needless to say that the Dover Castle was officially out-of-bounds during a shift but those stairs were well traversed.

Comparing the photographs of the Mews in wartime with several taken in 1999, very little has changed. The basic features still remain the same: at one end the building with windows that follow the ascent of the stairs, at the other the tall ones backing onto Harley Street. The Ambulance Station, located at the end of a side turning, was based in buildings with numbers from 25 to 42. It may be assumed that Hall Motors (of Paddington), occupying Nos. 37 to 42, was requisitioned as the nucleus around which to create Station 39. The No. 39 referred to the upstairs flat over the garages. (Reading through L.C.C. records one finds that a volunteer, J. A. Cross, applies to be attached to an Ambulance Station which he describes as being at Salmon's Garage, Shelton Street, W.C.2). *Kelly's Directory* for 1939 states that No. 32 housed the motor garage of John Burdock and John Angel & Sons, jobmasters, were at 44-45. Hall Garage at 41-42 also had an entrance fronting onto the other side of the Mews which afforded quick access in an emergency.

May remembered that "Pre-war the majority of dwellings above the Mews" garages had been occupied by chauffeurs and their families but by 1940 all had moved out except for a couple of Service families. In the flat next to the Station a commander in the Navy lived with his family. His wife was employed at John Lewis, the departmental store.

"I joined the London Auxiliary Ambulance Service on February 22nd, 1940 as a full-time crew member and served for five and a half years until the end of the war. Being aged thirty-seven, the government had required that I undertook an occupation that would assist the war effort. Although my husband, Jossie, advised the securing of a sedentary job in one of the government offices, I wanted to play a more active role. Living in St John's Wood I volunteered at the Ambulance Station in Lawn Road, Hampstead, and was assigned to the Auxiliary Ambulance Station 39, which was situated just off Weymouth Street in Weymouth Mews. Station 39 served an area bordered by Oxford Street to the south and Marylebone Road to the north. To the east was Tottenham Court Road with Edgware Road to the west. Regent's Park was included in the area.

"Having owned a car since 1926 meant that I had clocked up many years of motoring experience — the earliest driving licence that I have kept is dated 1933. Therefore I volunteered as an ambulance driver. Able-bodied men having joined the armed Services, women drivers were at a premium: far fewer women knew how to drive pre-war. Having been upgraded to Shift Leader, my friend, Elizabeth Bridge, captured several poses of

15

me displaying the two newly-acquired stripes on my arm denoting my new appointment. At that time she was working at a commercial photographic studio, before she went on to join the London Fire Service. I suspect that my career in teaching may have played a part in this promotion because having taught for many years I felt confident in my organisational skills and ability to lead personnel. By the first week of the Blitz I was further promoted to Deputy Station Officer.

"By 1942 I had been advanced to Station Officer, a post that I held until the end of hostilities in 1945 when the Station was closed. At the beginning of the war I received £1.18.9d a week which was increased later by one pound when I was promoted to Deputy Station Officer. When I became Station Officer a further pound was added which gave a total of £3.18.9d: a grand wage for a seventy-two or eighty-four hour week. Naturally any holidays granted were without pay."

According to the Minutes of the L.C.C. recorded at County Hall on October 10th, 1944, the three annual increases in rates of pay for a male driver with three year's experience compared with a female Station Officer meant that the driver earned 13/-a week more by this date. The conclusion was that these low rates of pay for females resulted in difficulties being experienced when attempting to fill vacancies due to the meagre recompense.

After May's death, Violet Black (who was one of her friends in London during the Blitz) wrote of her that "May's appointment must have been a wise decision by H.Q, for her proficiency, sense of fairness and discipline were the essential qualities needed to cope with various temperaments of colleagues, especially during the heaviest air raids."

HAND TORCHES ALLOWED

It was announced last night that to assist drivers and pedestrians in black-out conditions it has been decided to relax the present restrictions upon the use of headlamps in motor-vehicles and of hand torches by pedestrians. A suitable type of mask for headlamps has been devised by the Ministry of Home Security and will be placed on the market as soon as possible. When masks of this type are available their use will be compulsory on all vehicles on the roads at night. For the present, until the new mask is available, the following simple method of screening headlamps will be allowed under the lighting order:-

The bulb must be removed from the offside headlamp. An opaque cardboard disk must be fitted immediately behind the glass of the near side lamp, and must cover the whole area of the glass except for an aperture of a semi-circular shape 2in. in diameter, with the base uppermost. The centre of the base must coincide with the centre of the lamp. The lower part of the reflector must be completely blacked out e.g. with black cardboard or paper, or with two coats of matt black paint, up to a distance of half an inch above the centre line of the reflector.

The use of hand torches by pedestrians will be permitted subject to the following conditions:-

The light must be dimmed by placing two sheets of tissue paper or the equivalent over the glass bulb or the aperture through which the light is emitted. The light from the torch at all times must be projected downwards, and all torches must be extinguished during the period of an air-raid warning.

Pedestrians should bear in mind that it is difficult for drivers to see them at night, and the carrying of a white object, such as a newspaper or the wearing of a white article, such as a handkerchief, on the sleeve is recommended. Torches directed vertically downwards may be used by pedestrians to indicate their presence when crossing a road. They must never be directed towards a driver.

Attention is drawn to the fact that the use of headlamps and torches must cease as soon as an air raid warning is sounded: in such circumstances headlamps and torches must be extinguished immediately.

THE TIMES, SEPTEMBER 14th, 1939

May resumes: "Living in West Hampstead, travel to Weymouth Mews entailed a train journey followed by a walk of about half an hour. When I was on an eight-hour shift one change-over was at 23.30 which meant walking along totally blacked-out streets to or from the bus stop in Baker Street. People today can't register just how intense the darkness was when there was no moon. Even lakes were drained or covered with camouflage netting to disorientate enemy aircrews from using them as landmarks.

"The black-out was efficiently policed by the wardens who patrolled to make sure all sources of light were eliminated lest an enemy aircraft be guided by an errant beam. Traffic was only able to crawl because there was no street lighting and the use of normal headlights was forbidden. However the headlight had a louvred cover fitted which had an aperture the size of a shilling to allow a minute beam of light. Partially due to this fact, the speed limit for the ambulances was set at 16 m.p.h. Driving slowly over glass-strewn roads was mandatory lest a puncture occurred — a heinous crime. Pedestrians were also at considerable risk: my elder brother, Frank, walked straight into the corner of a brick air-raid shelter that had been erected in the centre of the pavement, knocking out all his front teeth.

"Some of the girls were nervous about this walk and were relieved when the change-over was adjusted to 08.00. Throughout all these years only one girl was assaulted on her way to the Station. Fortunately the attacker had chosen to tangle with a six-foot-tall ex-music hall artiste who managed to take care of herself. However she did arrive at the Station badly shaken: I told her it could have been worse." [This comment illustrates May's practical common sense: being sympathetic but quashing any fuss by looking at the problem from a different angle.]

May recalled that "one day cycling across Regent's Park on the way to the Station, I fell off splitting open my chin and flattening my nose. As I struggled to my feet, by good fortune there was a foreign doctor in the car behind me who came to my assistance. He examined my face and offered to take me to the nearest hospital. Explaining that I was en route to report for duty, I agreed only to be taken to a First Aid Post. Having patched up my face the staff asked if everywhere else felt all right, I remarked that the funny bone in my arm felt very strange whereupon they found a break above my elbow. This kind doctor drove me to the Middlesex Hospital where my arm was put in plaster and the wounds on my face stitched. On being taken home by car, I asked if we could drive through Regent's Park. There, seven hours after my accident, stood my bike propped against the railings. The next day, a Sunday, was my rest day but on Monday I returned to work with my arm in a sling. Jossie, who had not wanted me to enrol, was unsympathetic. During the six weeks my arm was in plaster, I found difficulty only in braiding my long hair as I wore it in a bun at the time.

"The staff at Station 39 fluctuated between eighty and eighty-five persons, of which a high percentage were women. At the beginning of the war there were about a dozen men on the staff but these were gradually reassigned to other services. However County Hall (where the headquarters of the London Ambulance Service was based) decreed that at least two men served on each shift. A wide cross-section of society was represented at the Station providing a unique mix of talents rarely to be found. For example there were several professional musicians including a concert pianist, a concert harpist and several accompanists, an art gallery owner, theatrical artistes, B.B.C. personnel (Langham Place was just down the road) besides a librarian, beauticians, dressmakers, shop assistants and, of course, housewives. A core of women, about forty in all, served with me there for the duration. These girls were great and I can recall many amusing incidents. Unfortunately as everyone was called by a surname, often I cannot recall their first names. I am still in touch with Babette Loraine (we both joined on the same day in February 1940) and Mary Rowley: sadly many others are now dead."

No records for the Auxiliary Service were known to survive until, in 1998, six individual foolscap files containing detailed records were discovered under the eaves in an attic at Brixton Ambulance Station. Then, in 1999, an incomplete set of card indexes for the L.A.A.S. were discovered in a basement at London Ambulance Service HQ at Waterloo. The cards do not give a complete list of auxiliaries because there are gaps in the alphabetical list. Moreover these individual cards give only limited information: full name and address, date of birth, entry and discharge dates, status, attendant or driver duties, reasons for leaving as well as any damage incurred to vehicles.

The six files, coated and stained with fifty years of dust and damp, belonged to personnel who had resigned, or in one case been dismissed, after serving from between sixteen days to five months early in the war. One folder bears the muddy imprint of a gum boot with a deep tread. Although these records were for full-time auxiliary drivers unconnected with Station 39, mention of them has been made because their files document the course of training common to all volunteers. The files

21

illustrate procedures in registering for National Service and chart the various tests and training meted out to Auxiliary Ambulance personnel. Thumbnail sketches vividly illustrate the volunteers' personalities and individual quirks. One left to marry much earlier than planned; another admitted to having flying experience and would have been transferred to the R.A.F. (although his Canadian mother may have been displeased); a third resigned having found the authoritarian attitude of the Station officers affected her quality of life, and another transferred to the South Eastern Station and his file was abandoned. The most intriguing records are for a taxi driver who gave cause for concern during the first and subsequent driving tests at headquarters. It was reported that the other personnel at his Station would not drive with him so he was instructed to drive a car alone at the head of a convoy. After four months he was dismissed in a tactful manner.

The National Service Act (Armed Forces) dated September 3rd, 1940, ushered in mandatory conscription for all males between the ages of eighteen and forty-one. Compulsory service for women was not introduced until December 1941, although like May, many joined up earlier. (By 1942 conscription was mandatory for all women born after 1900 so May would have been eligible.) At the beginning of the war there were 80,000 men enroled in the Civil Defence, but by 1941 this number had increased to 324,000 with 59,000 women joining the service. The following year saw a slight drop in the figures for men but an increase to 80,000 for women. The term Civil Defence encompassed the

Police, Ambulance Service, Fire Service, Rescue Services, Air Raid Wardens and was overseen by the Home Office and the Ministry for Home Security. The Home Secretary of the day was Herbert Morrison. During an "Incident" after a bomb had dropped, a central Control Room organised all the services tied in with an Incident Officer on the site.

Major F. A. L. de Gruchy reviews the build up of the Civil Defences in his *War Diary: An Overall War Picture, 1939-1945* published in 1949 which was based on lectures given to the Services during the war:

"By the middle of 1942 the organisation of life in Britain was geared to obtain maximum war effort. H.M. Government took over control of all manpower and resources. Peace time resources were adapted for war throughout industry. The replacement of men in industry and in the non-combatant duties of the forces and in most important Civil Defence had been carried out by the use of volunteers throughout the war. Compulsory service for women came in at the end of 1941 to enable the mobilisation of the last reserves.

"Civil defence was to all intents and purposes an integral part of the fighting services. Many whole-time workers and a large proportion of the population in part-time work assured the best counter measures for dealing with heavy air raids and prevented these raids from interfering with the war effort."

One file selected from the six discovered in the attic is that of Phyllis Cresswell, aged 26. It reveals that she volunteered to join the Ambulance Service on May 5th, 1939, by completing, "The Form of Application for

National Service". Phyllis entered details of her name, gave her age as twenty-six and her address as, "Hamsey Green Farm, Upper Warlingham, Surrey".

Although information was requested concerning present occupation and any previous job, this space was left blank. The form duly completed, she followed the instructions to fold as directed and address to the Service desired having ascertained the address from the National Service Guide. The form was sent to The Superintendent, South Western Ambulance Station, London Road, Stockwell, London, S. W.

All information concerning a volunteer was filed in a manilla folder which was kept at the area ambulance station which had responsibility for the specific auxiliary station. Frank Cresswell, joining in December 1939, was issued with a folder bearing his accession number, 3123, inscribed, "London County Council and Public Health Department". On blank lines below the titles were spaces for "Name", "Station" and "Status" — Frank was a driver. Various forms were glued onto the file including entries concerning absence and pay, etc. but in a later edition these grids were printed onto the card folder. Many of the later folders issued after 1939 were plain brown without titles.

Although May had volunteered solely to join the Auxiliary Ambulance Service, many women would have volunteered for the military services as well. Babette Loraine, for example, not wishing to be assigned to the army, had volunteered for the Wrens (Women's Royal Naval Service) and Waafs (Women's Auxiliary Air Force), as well as the Ambulance Service. The first reply she received was from the London County Council Ambulance Service who asked her to attend the Divisional Headquarters at Lawn Road for an interview, medical and tests. Her skills were checked in a test which included driving with a full pail of water on the floor in the footwell of the car. She passed and drove DXP 943, a Ford V8 van converted into an ambulance, at Station 39 for the duration of the war.

May explains that former military men, too old for active service, were assigned to the Ambulance Service where they were often promoted to senior posts. Younger men of military age who had failed their medical were drafted into the Ambulance Service early in the war but gradually they left when a more active role was found for them. Towards the end of the war the Station's full time crew of thirty was made up of women with the mandatory two men on each shift. Numbers, especially at night, would be augmented by part-timers who were either too old for military service or else in a job which excluded them from the call-up. The group photograph taken at the Station's closure, illustrates several men wearing ribbons denoting their active service during the previous war.

May remembers: "Men of military age who held conscientious objections to war were called before an Enquiry Board and offered non-combative duty. Many such men served in the Ambulance Service on the Home Front as well as in the Front Line. Our Station had two male "conchies" throughout the war: one was Alan Braley who wrote the poems featured later. In one [see page 105], he remarks that serving at Station 39 "is better far than going down a mine": another option for conchies. These two men had been transferred in late 1940, with my agreement, from another Station where they had undergone the hostility often meted out to "conchies"."

Besides full-time paid volunteers, the Ambulance Service enrolled unpaid part-time personnel. These would often be persons who worked in a regular paid job needed by the war effort but who could be called upon in an emergency. Stephanie Currie (neé Jones), a volunteer from Watford, worked on bombers by day and as a volunteer several nights a week. Due to their expertise some people were especially well qualified to assist the Service on a part-time basis. H. C. Toms' taxi driving skills and his "Knowledge" (the detailed memorising of the London area which is still a mandatory acquisition for all taxi drivers) ensured that his presence was prized at Station 39; doubly so since May 1940 when all signposts and direction indicators together with street names had been removed. Everyday the personnel had topographical exercises so that when an emergency call came they could respond immediately by finding their route within the designated area: Oxford Street to the south, Marylebone Road to the north, Tottenham Court Road to the east and Edgware Road to the west. Journeys outside their area sometimes necessitated having a lead car, often a taxi, to show the way.

Babette was reminded that Toms either could not or would not reverse the vehicle he was driving. Taxis would usually execute a U-turn in the road if they needed to turn round, so, presumably, it was a sign of his status not to reverse when instructed to do so. From another reminiscence one can assume that maybe topography was not the most exciting of subjects. During a questionnaire on the subject, Joan Davies walked into the room carrying a Lilo which she proceeded to blow up, while totally ignoring the class. She placed the Lilo under the table and promptly went to sleep: taking refuge under a table was recommended as a precaution against bomb blast during an emergency. Joan, a well-known concert pianist, had a mind of her own in common with many of these mature professional women. Although all staff were expected to scrub the concrete floors, Joan's floor cleaning duties were shared out amongst her colleagues in order to ensure her hands were protected for the audiences at the Albert Hall.

Early in 1940, Stephanie Currie volunteered for the Women's Land Army but having had a childhood problem with her hip was not accepted. She was directed to a job repairing damaged Wellington bombers by day but also volunteered to be on standby at the Watford Ambulance Station by night. She muses that she must have been very fit to be able to lift the heavy stretchers up onto the upper position in the ambulances. Stephanie explains the conditions required to be accepted as an unpaid volunteer driver:

"Initially volunteers had to qualify on a St John Ambulance or Red Cross first aid course which normally ran for between six and eight weeks. As I wished to be enrolled as a driver, I took instruction with the R.A.C. which set a stringent test. I was assigned to Watford

Ambulance Station, which was based off Bushey Mill Lane. [A second station was based at Ashleigh House between Watford and Croxley Green.] When I was summoned by a knock on the door, I would cycle down to the yard where all the ambulances were parked. The first person to arrive had to collect the keys from a neighbouring building. There was no precise time when I would be called upon as the demand was controlled by the scale of bombing as well as the personnel available within the London region. At Watford we were only called upon when a specific London area was unable to mount a force large enough to deal with the estimated victims. Due to distance from London and the shortage of petrol, it was one of the last stations to be called upon. London Control Centre instructed Watford where to send us, generally to an Ambulance Station, often Station 39, from where we would be redirected to the scene. Our route to London was always along the Watford bypass onto the Edgware Road to Marble Arch and either to Regent Street or Marylebone Road.

"Being volunteers who worked during the day meant that we were not expected to work any specific time. The plan was to spread the load so that volunteers could continue with their daytime jobs. For example I would be called out, literally by someone knocking on my door, who then ran on to alert the next volunteer. Call-out would be up to three times in one week with possibly a further four times in the following week. My work in the day time during 1941-1942 was from 7.30a.m. until 7.30p.m. so I would not be available before 8.30p.m. The length of any call-out would be dependent on a variety of factors. No food was provided. If a siren sounded during our drive to London, we were instructed to park the ambulance and proceed to the nearest shelter or underground station and await the "all-clear" before continuing. The ambulances, being conversions of commercial vans, were extremely uncomfortable with little springing. It was necessary to double declutch through the gears. During the Blitz, London was bombed every night until the Christmas Eve when a lull lasted until New Year's Eve when incendiary bombs were dropped.

"No one seems to think about the trauma involved. It was not impossible to find a rat-eaten body lying behind a wall that had been upright the last time the district had been visited. Worse would be driving the delivery of separated limbs to the refrigerators in Billingsgate Fish Market — the largest in London. I would not eat fish for years afterwards. Here the limbs would be stored prior to efforts being made to identify the victim by birth mark, tattoo or previous incapacity. Never had I realised the dead weight of a limb. Directors never seem to show that sort of task in any of their films, merely the drama and the glamour. This exposure to trauma was voluntary; no pay was involved, just tiredness and the struggle to keep awake the following day to do your regular job."

May's friend, Violet Black, "Blackie", serving as a volunteer, was for a time based at the Fire Service Area Headquarters near Manchester Square. As the Incident Reports show, this Station covered the same area as Station 39. During the Blitz in 1940 she remembered that as many as three hundred enemy aircraft would

29

bomb London every night. This constant assault lasted for fifty-seven consecutive nights. Of the bombs that were dropped she recalled that incendiary bombs would be deployed initially to ignite and give illumination of the targets. High explosive bombs would follow as well as oil-filled bombs that ignited on impact. A further hazard was the land mine which floated down on a parachute until a solid object was reached. During September 1940 the press carried reports of "Molotov Bread-baskets" bursting over the City. The bombs seemed to be of a new type since they exploded with a vivid white flash followed by a sharp crack. A succession of staccato reports followed like machine-gun fire. On the night of September 12th over a hundred Londoners died.

After completing the "National Service Application Form" requesting to join the Service, an applicant filled in a form entitled "L.C.C. Public Health Department, L.A.S. Air Raid Precautions, Application for Enrolment as a Volunteer Ambulance Driver". The form requested, name, age, address and telephone number. Questions were included on length of driving experience and availability for service in a chosen area of London. Phyllis Cresswell indicated that she was willing to serve in any part of the capital and that she was prepared to learn first aid and anti-gas precautions.

It is interesting to note on the reverse of that form applicants had to sign that they agreed to the "Conditions of Service for Volunteers". They accepted "The Air-raid Precautions Service for whole or part-time Service in War" regulations formulated by the Home

Office. They were to be natural-born British subjects willing to undertake the prescribed course of training. Volunteers were required to present themselves if an emergency arose and to act under the directions of the authority's officers. Only full-time volunteers received pay with a week's notice of termination either way. Two sections dealing with "Compensation payable for incapacity resulting from active duty", to a widow and dependent children or dependent relatives, "will be in accordance with the terms specified". Furthermore the form stated that, "in time of war, compensation will be payable under conditions determined at the time for both part and full-time in the case of death or disablement". Phyllis has signed an undertaking that she has read the conditions and will serve in the London Volunteer Ambulance Service, later to be renamed the Auxiliary Ambulance Service. The form was duly returned to County Hall, S.E.1.

By mid-1940 this form had been amended to exclude the offer of compensation, instead stating that sick pay was administered by the Ministries of Pensions or Home Security in accordance with the Personal Injuries (Emergency Provisions) Act, 1939. Payment for sickness or injury sustained in the course of duty were now stringently restricted, being paid only in "special circumstances". Furthermore, auxiliaries (the term volunteers had been replaced throughout the form) absent from duty without permission would render themselves liable to dismissal. The second edition of this form incorporates a section for next-of-kin and the space for two referees names, addresses and occupations. A letter from the Medical Officer of Health, based at County Hall explained the new conditions.

No. 3123, volunteer Frank Cresswell, has a letter in his file dated February 26th, 1940 from Dr Norman Gurrie stating that he was suffering from, "Lumbar fibrositis". A further letter informs that he was fit to resume work. The relevant entry on his record file notes, "no sick pay allowed". It is of interest to read that Frank moved house from 29 to 93 Stockwell Green, S.W.9. before moving to 347 Brixton Road in the same area. One may speculate that the bombing had left him doubly homeless.

A foolscap sheet entitled "L.C.C., London Ambulance Service, Air Raid Precautions, Volunteer Ambulance Drivers" contains the comments entered by the examiner after the applicant had taken a driving test. Superintendent H. Saunders, a retired Station Officer obviously called back to war service, finds Phyllis Cresswell's driving ability on May 6th, 1939, "very good," but notes that her first-aid and mechanical knowledge is nil although she has a degree of proficiency in running repairs. Her physique is good and she should become, "an ambulance driver with first-aid knowledge and capability for handling loaded stretchers".

The information gleaned from this initial driving test and future practice and tests was entered on "L.A.S. Volunteer Section". On the card of Mrs Rona Crichlow, designated a W. T. driver, it is noted that her husband, Dr Crichlow, worked for the Ministry of Health at the Emergency Headquarters at Aylesbury. In fact Rona's card has over a page of detailed entries concerning tests and including absences from duty. Obviously at Station 65 during the early days of the war in 1939 there was plenty of time to keep records up-to-date. For example, three driving lessons were taken on consecutive days in July and administered by Instructor Gregory. He comments after 30, 60 and 50-minute drives that she, "needs confidence". As she only covered seven miles in one hour maybe he was nervous too. However a month later, Instructor Harding notes that she shows improvement but next day Gregory merely notes the three miles were driven in a Ford. November's outings are in a Ford but not until late in the month does Gregory agree that her sight is good as well as her driving. Unfortunately no further mention is made of her driving prowess but her absence due to sickness is noted. By December 29th, Rona had resigned.

Babette Loraine serving at Station 39 remembers taking a driving test at Lawn Road Ambulance Station (the North-Western London Ambulance Service HQ) which included driving with a full pail of water on the floor of the car to check on the ease with which gears were changed: many commercial vehicles required lengthy double declutching to select each gear change. Having passed this aspect of the test, she had to accompany a regular ambulance driver as his attendant for several journeys in order to acquire the feel of the job and practice in real life. She remembers an early call out: a young man had fallen out of the window in a block of flats and impaled himself on the railings. The driver thoughtfully said she need not join in the body's removal: not a pleasant task. Driving straight to the mortuary, she experienced more shocks. The doctor enquired of her if she would be interested to see some of his work. He unwrapped a body which had been stitched up and waited for her approval!

Joan Pannell (she and Babette were the younger of the crew members at Station 39) left about 1942 to join the Wrens. Babette mentioned wistfully that she expected her friend had a more exciting time in the Wrens!

LONDON AMBULANCE SERVICE AS AT FEBRUARY 1944

GENERAL SECTION

Station	Address
Western	Allen Mansions, Allen Street, W.8.
	12 Phillimore Terrace, W.8.
North-Western	Lawn Road, Hampstead, N.W.3.
	22 Lawn Road, N.W.3. (A.S.Q.)
Eastern	Brooksby's Walk, Homerton, E.9.
Brook	Shooter's Hill Road, Greenwich, S.E.18.
South-Eastern	New Cross Road, Deptford, S.E.14.
South-Western	Landor Road, S.W.9.

ACCIDENT SECTION

Western (A)	Seagrave Road, Fulham, S.W.6.
Bloomsbury (B)	19 Herbrand Street, Tavistock Place, W.C.1.

Shoreditch (C)   Basing House Yard, Kingsland Road, E.2.
Lee (D)   142 High Road, Lee, S.E.13.
South Western (E) Landor Road, S.W.9.
Elephant and
    Castle (F)   15 St. George's Market, London Road, S.E.1.
Poplar (G)   7 Woolmore Street, E.14.
Highbury (H)   Corsica Street, Highbury, N.5.
Paddington (K)   Lyons Place, St. John's Wood, N.W.8.
Battersea (L)   119 Battersea Rise, S.W.11.
Woolwich (M)   High Street, Woolwich, S.E.18.
Westminster (O) 93 Regency Street, S.W.1.
Old Kent Road (P) 301 Ilderton Road, S.E.15.
Hackney (R)   Paragon Road, Mare Street, E.9.
Streatham (S)   Mountearl Gardens, S.W.16.
North
 Kensington (T) Silchester Mews, North Kensington, W.10.
Headquarters   3-5 Lambeth Palace Road, S.E.1.

AUXILIARY STATIONS

2   41 Munster Road, S.W.6. (Vehicles)
    Cobham Lodge, 37 Munster Road, S.W.6. (Staff)
1   16, 18 & 20a Avonmore Road, W.11.
6   164-6 Fulham Palace Road, W.6.
9   72 Black Lion Lane, W.6. (Vehicles)
    1 St. Peter's Square, W.6. (Staff)
11   1-16 Wood Lane, W.12.

12	65-83 Queen Caroline Street, W.6.
14	Prince's Yard, 3 Princedale Road, W.ll. (Vehicles)
	5 Norland Square, W.11. (Staff)
17	2, 3 & 5 Logan Mews, W.8. (Vehicles)
	Garden Lodge, Logan Place, W.8. (Staff)
19	Lex Garage 7 Pembridge Villas, W.11. (Vehicles)
	6 Pembridge Villas, W.11. (Staff)
23	85-89 King's Road, S.W.3.
24	Barnsale Garage, Barnsdale Road, W.9. (Vehicles)
	35 Elgin Avenue, W.9. (Staff)
26	1-10 Conduit Mews, W.2. (Vehicles)
	12, 13 & 14 Conduit Mews, W.2. (Staff)
28	1, 6, 7 & 13 Fulton Mews, W.2. (Vehicles)
	26 Porchester Terrace, Bayswater Road, W.2. (Staff)
32	Northways Garage, Finchley Road, N.W.3. (Vehicles) (corner of College Cres.)
	145 Finchley Road, N.W.3. (Staff)
33	33 Hampstead High Street, N.W.3.
34	Mill Lane Garages, 160 Mill Lane, N.W.6. (Vehicles)
	1 & 2 Cavendish Mansions, N.W.6. (Staff)
37	466/490 Edgware Road, W.2. and Flat 3 Kingsbury House, Edgware Road, W.2.
39	35/42 Weymouth Mews, W.1. (Vehicles)
	16 Weymouth Mews, W.1. (Staff)
40	Flats 36, 39 and 40 Kingston House, Kensington Road, S.W.7.
	Kingston House Garage

41	28 Bruton Place, W.1. and 29 Bruton Street, W.1.
42	Adelphi, Savoy Place, W.C.2.
44	Dolphin Square Garage, Grosvenor Road, S.W.1. (Vehicles)
	Rooms 49/52 Beatty House, Flat 06 Beatty House; and Rooms 1/4 Raleigh House (Ground Floor), Dolphin Square, S.W.1. (Staff)
50	20/22 William Road, N.W.1.
51	23/24 Starcross Street, N.W.1.
55	Brookfield Garages, St. Alban's Road, N.W.5. (Vehicles)
	30 Swain's Lane, N.W.5. and 18 St. Alban's Road, N.W.5. (Staff)
56A	Russell Court, 3-16 Woburn Place, W.C.1.
58	6/9 Upper St. Martin's Lane, W.C.2.
59	447/449 Holloway Road, N.7.
61	217 & 219/227 Caledonian Road, N.1.
65	Cooksey & Sons' Garage, Compton Avenue, N.1. (Vehicles)
	7 Compton Terrace, N.1. (Staff)
66	394 Camden Road, N.7. (Vehicles)
	291A Camden Road, N.7. (Staff)
67	1A Finsbury Park Road, N.4. (Vehicles)
	298A Seven Sisters Road, N.4. (Staff)
70	79/89 Pentonville Road, N.1.
73	42, 45, 72 & 103-5 The Minories, E.C.3.
74	Cameron Wharf, Greenwich Street, E.C.4. (Vehicles)
	No. 4 Joiners' Hall Buildings, Upper Thames Street, E.C.4. (Staff)

77	City of London Eastern Ambulance Station, New Street, Bishopsgate, E.C.2.
78	City of London Western Ambulance Station, West Smithfield, E.C.1.
80	Olympic House, 42 Newington Green, N.16. and Elm Tree Works, 1-21 (odd), Albion Road, N.16.
82	92 Stamford Hill, N.16. (Vehicles) 90 Stamford Hill, N.16. (Staff)
84	449 Kingsland Road, E.8. (Vehicles) 39 Lea Bridge Road, E.5. (Staff)
86	35-37 Lea Bridge Road, E.5. (Vehicles) 39 Lea Bridge Road, E.5. (Staff)
89	18-20 Urswick Road, E.9. and Upton House L.C.C. Central School, Urwick Road, E.9.
90	Edmund Halley L.C.C. School, Orsman Road, N.1. and Flats 42, 45 & 46, Longbow House, Mill Row, N.1.
91	188 Haggerston Road, E.8.
97	78-86 Mansford Street, E.2. (Vehicles) 31-32 Nelson Gardens, E.2. (Staff)
98	130-131 Three Colts Lane, E.2. (Vehicles) Stewart Headlam L.C.C. School, Somerford Street, E.1. (Staff)
101	Trafalgar L.C.C. School, Trafalgar Gardens, White Horse Lane, E.1.
103	147 Cannon Street Road, E.1.
104	D & W Gibbs, Brewhouse Lane, E.1.
106	Market Garage, 25 Spital Square, E.1.
109	24 & 24A Bow Road, E.3.

111   Bullivant's Wharf, West Ferry Road, E.14.

112   Morton's Yard, West Ferry Road, E.14 and
413 West Ferry Road, E.14

114   Far Famed Cake Co. Rifle Street, E.14.

115   Ancona Road L.C.C. School, S.E.18.

117   43 King's Highways, S.E.18.
46 Southend Crescent, Eltham, S.E.9.

118   58 Eltham High Street, S.E.9.

119   160/162 Powis Street, S.E.18. (Vehicles)
156 & 158 Powis Street, S.E.18. (Staff)

126   Christ's College, St. German's Place, Blackheath,
S.E.3.

128   246 Bromley Road, S.E.6.

129   170 & 172 Lee High Road, S.E.13.

137   54 Dacres Road, S.E.23.

139   Tower Bridge Junior L.C.C. School, Fair Street,
S.E.1.

141   Peter Hills School, Rupack Street, Brunel Road,
S.E.16.

143   Mary Ann Buildings, Deptford High Street,
S.E.8.

144   2A Shardeloes Road, S.E.14. (Vehicles), and
60 Lewisham Way, S.E.14. (Staff)

145   "Medina," adjoining 1 Breakspears Road, S.E.4.
(Vehicles)
11 Breakspears Road, S.E.4. (Staff)

148   179/191 Borough Hill Street, S.E.1.
Chapel Court, Borough High Street, S.E.1.

149   Walworth L.C.C. Central School, Mina Road,
S.E.17.

159   73A Dulwich Village, S.E.21 (Vehicles)
4 Court Lane, S.E.21 (Staff)

161	1 Zenoria Street, S.E.23 (Vehicles) 14 Lordship Lane, S.E.22. (Staff)
163	63 Denmark Hill, S.E.5. (Vehicles) 67 Denmark Hill, S.E.5. (Staff)
167	Cormont Road L.C.C. School, Myatt's Fields, S.E.5
168	40-44 Norwood Road, S.E.24 (Vehicles) 36 Norwood Road, S.E.24 (Staff)
170	77 & 79 Clapham Road, S.W.9.
171	260 Knight's Hill, S.E.27 (Vehicles) 217 Knight's Hill, S.E.27 (Staff)
174	332-338, Clapham Road, S.W.9. (Vehicles) 328 Clapham Road, S.W.9. (Staff)
178	326 Queenstown Road, S.W.8.
179	16/18 Westbridge Road, S.W.11. (Vehicles) Bolingbroke L.C.C. School, Bolingbroke Walk, S.W.11. (Staff)
180	Honeywell Road L.C.C. School, S.W.11.
181	2, 4 & 6 Althorp Road, S.W.17. (Vehicles) 24 Bellevue Road, S.W.17. (Staff)
188	43 Mitcham Lane, S.W.16 (Vehicles) 66 Babington Road, S.W.16. (Staff)
191	Garratt Lane L.C.C. School, S.W.18.
196	257 Upper Richmond Road, S.W.15. (Vehicles) 253 Upper Richmond Road, S.W.15. (Staff)
198	260 Balham High Road, S.W.17. (Vehicles) 268 Balham High Road, S.W.17. (Staff)
200	74 Park Hill, S.W.4. (Vehicles) 87 Park Hill, S.W.4. (Staff)
T.S.2	6 & 12 Kendrick Place, 14 Kendrick Mews and 18 Reece Mews, S.W.7.

T.S.3   29 Riley Street, S.W.10, and World's End Studios,
        5 & 6 Apollo Place, S.W.10.
        112 Cheyne Walk, S.W.10.

T.S.1   Trafalgar Garage, Park Row, S.E.10. (Vehicles)
        Flats 4 & 5 Trafalgar Tavern, Park Rows, S.E.10. (Staff)

T.S.5   7 & 8 Prince Albert Road, N.W.1.

CHAPTER
THREE

Weymouth Mews

Station 39 covered an area which incorporated four large garages each capable of accommodating four ambulances. Walking down from the entrance in Weymouth Street, towards New Cavendish Street at the far end, the Station's premises lay down the cul-de-sac mid-way along on the right-hand side and in a recess to the left. These garages, Nos. 32 to 38 together with 41 to 43 at right angles, were formerly the business premises of Hall Motors. The latter garage afforded through access into the eastern leg of the Mews: allowing a rapid response and a clear, quick route in an emergency. The stairway on the right of the garage gave easy access to the Dover Castle, maybe equally important.

Turning into the recess, the garage on the north side had been converted into a recreational room containing a ping-pong table and a piano. At one end office area had been partitioned off and contained cupboards, table, three chairs and the safe. The vital telephone, the link with Control in any raid, had pride of place.

The flat over the garages housed the rest rooms, canteen, common room and two bathrooms. Babette, an auxiliary, remembers how panic reigned the day that a rat eluded pursuers, raced into the bathroom and installed itself in the Geyser water heater. Unfortunately the heater was alight and the rat met a nasty death. One of the men disposed of the body down the pan later in the day. The stairs to the flat had to be scrubbed every day in strict rota system.

May explains: "The eighty personnel were divided into two alternating shifts, which contained a nucleus of staff through the duration. Initially at the beginning of the war there were eight-hour shifts, but later twelve-hour shifts were introduced and finally twenty-four hour shifts. Either the Station Officer would be in charge of a shift or the Deputy Station Officer: both wore three stripes but the former displayed one pip. A Shift Leader, sporting two stripes, was assigned to be responsible for each shift, assisted by the Leading Hand with a single stripe. The final system meant that crews were on call throughout the twenty-four hours. If an emergency was developing then they would be expected to extend their duty.

"If there was a lull then the crews were allowed to relax in the common room on a rota system, although the quality of relaxation was minimal since there were only a few deck chairs and, as the photographs show, one Lloyd Loom chair. When the weather was fine we sat outside in the Mews: many such photos exist, one is captioned wistfully, "Waiting for the Tide to come in". Here we read, sewed, knitted for the men of the H.M.S. *Corfield* or played cards.

"In the early days of the war, before my promotion, I painted scenes from the windows. At night we rested as best we could on the concrete floor, later we brought in Lilos. When the air raid shelter had been built in the Mews, six beds were available there for use, but I prided myself that I never went inside any shelter for the duration of the war."

The sole interior illustration of Station 39 which has survived shows Station Officer Butler peering through the message hatchway. From this aperture the chits would be handed out to crews designated to respond to an emergency. The attendant would await the chit while the driver would start the ambulance: response time was within two minutes.

May explains that early in 1940, the Station had six ambulances, four cars and a single decker Green Line bus. Four of the ambulances were Fords with V8 engines, one was a Chrysler and the other a Studebaker. The latter vehicles had been converted to carry the wounded by adding a box van body with fittings for four stretchers. These ambulances afforded a most uncomfortable ride for both patient and attendant, whether sitting or lying down. No auxiliary stations were fortunate enough to possess the purpose-built Talbot white ambulances. They were built by Clement-Talbot Ltd in conjunction with W. & G. DuCros of Acton. In the mid-1930s they produced them on special 6-cylinder chassis with pre-selector gearbox and double-reduction rear axle.

There are several photographs depicting lines of cars and ambulances with each driver, and attendant in the case of ambulances, standing smartly alongside. Vehicles were lined up for inspection or in preparation to join a convoy. Each bears the inscription L.C.C. Ambulance St Marylebone with the specific vehicle number allocated. May remembered that Regular Ambulance Service Officers from County Hall would arrive to carry out an inspection wearing special white gloves with which to test for any dirt lodged, for example, under the wings.

May continues: "Some of these large and expensive cars had been presented to the Ambulance Service by Government departments and foreign embassies: petrol shortage and subsequent rationing, and in some cases being on the opposing side, had curtailed their journeys. (Renovating a pre-war Wolseley in 1994, the writer discovered that it had been stored up on blocks in the cellars of the British Embassy in Paris for the duration.) A Rolls-Royce acquired by the Service had belonged to the renowned Lady Docker. The Minutes of June 10th, 1940, record the gift of two motor ambulances being presented to the L.A.A.S. from the Ambulance Trust Fund.

"Petrol, issued in green five-gallon cans, was stored in the garages: creating no doubt, a serious fire risk. Looking at my colleagues, captured on film smoking cigarettes and pipes, maybe we were fortunate not to have a local emergency to deal with. Eily Airey was never without a cigarette and even the L.A.S Instructor is to be observed smoking his pipe while lecturing on engine maintenance. Being severely rationed, petrol was allocated solely for priority users which necessitated a mandatory picket. All the vehicles' engines were checked by starting them twice in each shift to ensure a rapid response in an emergency. An officer, carrying out an audit during a quiet period of the war, discovered a discrepancy between the mileage logged for the Studebaker and the petrol used. I was questioned on the "missing" two gallons of petrol and found myself having to explain that the huge engine drank petrol every time it was started, even though it had not been driven an inch. Not only did starting these huge engines use up petrol, it was no wonder that their batteries suffered too."

"Not until we were placed on twenty-four hour shifts were we provided with any food or refreshment on the Station. From time to time the gas or water supplies would be cut off due to the bombing or because of the threat from further explosions. However nothing was allowed to interfere with our sense of duty and joining in to beat Hitler. Both shifts were expected to carry out thorough cleaning duties not only inside the station but also on all the vehicles. When a shift changed the two Shift Leaders would inspect every aspect of the Station carefully before the incoming leader would accept and sign the transfer."

Babette Loraine explained that she usually drove Ambulance DXP 943, a converted Ford. Her attendant was usually a girl who could not drive and who became very agitated in emergencies: not the best choice of assistant. On one occasion, she recalls being called out of their usual area into south-west London. Driving very slowly, the engine stalled alongside a "Road Blocked" sign announcing an unexploded bomb. Her attendant panicked.

For a period of six months during term-time, Babette had the routine duty to ferry, in a Green Line bus, a party of disabled local children to and from their special school in Elgin Avenue. This duty meant nearly two hours of driving twice a day. The bus had to be cleaned inside and out at the end of both journeys. Trundling along the roads in pea-soup fogs, Babette recalled the difficulties as she and her attendant tried to recognise the mothers waiting patiently at the shrouded kerb-side for their children to be returned. Besides the usual causes of fog, many cities employed dustbins sporting lids incorporating chimneys which were placed at regular intervals along the kerbs. At dusk the contents of these "smoke screens" would be set alight and the ensuring thick pall of burning oil would produce a throat-choking fog: excellent for confusing would-be bombers but especially disastrous for asthma sufferers.

Babette recalled how, during a raid, a colleague was sent upstairs to persuade an old lady suffering from asthma to abandon her damaged home. The woman categorically refused to allow the auxiliary to lead her to safety, explaining that her husband had always said she must not go out if atmosphere was smoky. An impasse being reached, the auxiliary drove to fetch a doctor. The medic's stern advice immediately caused the old lady to acquiesce to being taken to hospital.

May writes that the bus was kept at the garage together with the Station's school ambulance. These vehicles would be used to ferry other stations' crews to and from the A.R.P. School at Highbury although interruptions and emergencies often curtailed these assignments. Other intermittent duties included the collection of dirty laundry from about nine stations in the area for delivery to Lawn Road, their local Headquarters, on Mondays, clean laundry being collected and distributed to the same stations on the return journey. On Wednesdays it might be their turn on the rota to collect the completed pay sheets from the other nine stations and deliver them to the M. W. Pay Office. On alternate Thursdays the storekeeper collected a fortnight's supply of stores from M.W. Ambulance Station.

May remembers that "at the beginning of the war, a temporary wall was fitted across a section of one garage to provide an office. The office, the hub of the Station, was run by two officers, Misses Bruce and Fisher. An emergency call having been received from Central Control by the auxiliary on duty, crew details and their destination would be written on a chit. A decision would be made by the officer on the number of ambulances and cars required to respond. This procedure completed, the attendants were handed their instructions on a chit through the message hatch while the driver started the ambulance. The Station prided itself that within two minutes the vehicles would be on their way to the incident. Walking wounded were ferried to the nearest hospital by car and stretcher cases by ambulance. Assignment completed, the crews would drive immediately back to Station 39 ignoring any further incidents en route to which other crews would have been allocated.

"In October 1940, Miss Bruce and Gweneth Fisher decided to resign their posts due to the fact that the Station had no air raid shelter. [A terse comment, heavily underlined, on Fisher's index card notes, "Last day of duty, 3.10.1940".] Being responsible for receiving emergency messages and deploying the crews, they would have been expected to stay in the office and not resort to shelters. The phone rang on the evening in question as I prepared to travel to the Station. The Inspector instructed me not to report for duty that night as the Station was closed but to present myself in the morning at 9a.m. (I found out subsequently that they had simply locked the office and gone home.) Having explained the situation to my husband, Jossie replied in his typical chauvinist fashion: 'That's women's service for you. Thank God, we still have the Navy.'

"Arriving at Station 39 in the morning", May continues, "I was promoted to Acting Station Officer."

Babette remembers the day when "our telephone at 39 broke down one evening, consequently every time we wanted to make contact with Control, the official wardens or other official posts, we had to run to Portland Place, a little distance away. We were sent in turn as quickly as possible to carry and receive urgent information, wearing our tin hats and carrying our gas masks. Our own guns in Regent's Park were popping into the skies after enemy aircraft. Showers of shrapnel fell with a "ping" to the ground all around. No need to remind "runners" to run quickly. We collected pieces of shrapnel as souvenirs, often before they were cool."

May recalls that "during emergencies, our Station usually operated within the given area but sometimes we were sent further afield if bombing was heavy elsewhere. On several occasions we were sent to railway stations to collect the wounded from the trains. When there was no alert, the Station undertook routine accident and transport work to and from hospitals using the ambulances or cars."

In 1939, volunteer applicants were asked to name the regional ambulance station at which they wished to train.

May remarked that the L.C.C. officials "were not used to having a large majority of women on station". She believed they were "over-awed" by some highly articulate professional women who were at the peak of their careers. Although these women were addressed solely by their surname, this fact did nothing to obscure their inbred authority and class. Jokes were made at the expense of some of the more pompous officials. The crews, lined up to attention by their vehicles, found it amusing to watch the inspectors checking for mud under each car in such a serious manner.

May remembers that "on entering the service the full-time staff were given a course with lectures on first aid providing there was no emergency. In my possession I have three certificates which were awarded for proficiency in First Aid and Civil Defence. My member's card shows that I belonged to the St Marylebone Civil Defence Services Association. The card is numbered 1310 and signed by S. Parker Bird the Honorary Secretary. I have also kept my Identity Card and many of my driving licences but find the first extant is 1933."

Volunteers were covered by the "Conditions of Service" formulated by the War Office. The pre-war version was printed on the reverse of the, "Application for Enrolment" form. The conditions stipulated that a volunteer incapacitated while training (or if he should die his widow plus dependent children or even relatives) would receive compensation, "in accordance with the terms notified". Both full-time and part-time volunteers would be compensated if they were killed or disabled in the course of wartime duty. However within a few months of war being declared, these generous conditions for compensation were withdrawn in a letter signed by the Medical Officer of Health for the L.C.C. on November 22nd, 1939, which referred to the "Personal Injuries (Emergency Provisions) Act, 1939". Anyone wishing their case for compensation to be heard had to make application to the Unemployment Assistance Board backed up with a medical certificate from their own doctor. A further rule stipulated that injury allowances were only granted after a minimum absence from duty of seven consecutive days due to the injury.

Stephanie Currie, the part-time volunteer based at Watford, describes treating victims:

"The first aid practised by the volunteers was in essence different from the basic St John's course which I had already completed. We were instructed to rescue with all due speed and, after a quick assessment of the patient's injuries, prevent further damage. As the patients would be taken to hospital immediately there was no need to dress superficial wounds or spend time applying elaborate bandages. Broken legs were stabilised in a rudimentary fashion by tying them together at the knees and ankles with arm slings. If necessary the patient would be tied down to the bunk with elastic bandages to eliminate further damage. In the event of the intestines being exposed we were instructed to cover the abdomen with our tin hats "to keep infection out and the guts in". [Maybe this plain speaking was aimed at shocking the more aristocratic ladies. Certainly one auxiliary remembers with horror the description of the procedure to follow in dealing with childbirth. She worried lest in cutting the cord she would endanger mother and child. However May was not easy to upset or shock.]

"Where necessary we quickly applied field dressings. Arriving at hospital, the nurses would replace our initial dressings with their own. These dirty dressings were retrieved and placed in a bag to take home for washing and re-rolling. Although an unpleasant task, it ensured that the cost of dressings was kept to the minimum. Bandage rolling is a lost art in the hospitals of today."

May recalls that "when I was appointed as Station Officer, I was sent to New End Hospital to observe operations. The sister, showing me around the theatre while explaining procedure, looked askance when I asked her why there was no bucket underneath the operating table to collect the blood. As girls, my sister Kathleen and I had watched when pigs were killed in the village's backyards, a bucket being placed beneath the slab to collect the blood." [This horrible tale was repeated to the author with relish by Kathleen, May's sister, who was also a nurse.] "I also had to attend demonstrations on how to strip down engines and reassemble them. It might be thought this would be of more use that watching operations, however it was judged to be too dangerous to allow us to carry out any repairs or alterations to the engines so I cannot imagine why I was sent on this course.

"The driver assigned to an ambulance was responsible for checking water, oil, petrol and lights at the start of each shift every single day between 9.30 and 10.30a.m. For this purpose the driver kept a rough log book to record fillings of petrol, water and oil together with mileage covered and incidental entries to cover bulb replacements and suchlike sundries. The data from this rough log would be entered in the regulation log book kept for the vehicle by the Shift Leader. Both driver and attendant were required to clean the ambulance daily: a photo shows a ladder propped against the side for this purpose. Usually the driver cleaned the engine and polished the bonnet, wings and cabin while the attendant washes the interior of the ambulance checking the fittings. When the Station was undermanned, one team had to cover several vehicles. Although the whole procedure is followed every day, certain specific duties were carried out on different days of the week."

Driving accompanied by their attendant, they had to observe a speed limit of sixteen miles an hour. This may seem to be inordinately slow but there was the constant danger of ruining tyres on the glass-strewn roads. The most heinous crime was to puncture a tyre as the import of rubber had been affected by the war: remoulds were only available for priority users.

May recounted that one of their drivers, Christina Finlay, in a reckless mood drove through broken glass and had shredded all her tyres by the time she returned to Station. Asked why she did this, she replied there was a crowd in her way and that she was in a hurry. There was no excuse for tyre damage as the reply was always: "You must have been driving too fast". However when a driver tried to limit the speed of the loaded ambulance to below sixteen miles an hour there was always the possibility of the engine boiling which would mean a delay while it cooled.

Stephanie recounts how she lost "her" ambulance: "Sally, my attendant, and I were driving along the Edgware Road returning to our Watford Station following a call-out to Central London when a warden shouted to us, 'Your back's on fire!' At that time the ambulances were flat-backed lorries to which had been added a canvas cover. Inside were four wooden bunk beds usually two each side. The use of wood plus the fact that the petrol tank was at the rear meant that any such fire would quickly get out of control: this happened in our case. We halted, jumped out of the vehicle when, almost simultaneously, the tank exploded. Returning to Watford by train via Euston railway station, we reported that our ambulance was lost. The initial response was, 'How on the earth could you do that?' An hour and a half's interrogation followed: today it would be called a debriefing."

Damage to vehicles was recorded on the reverse of the index cards and a reference number given. May's card records that an incident occurred on 9.10.1940, (in the week she took over as Acting Station Officer due to the resignation of Bruce and Fisher) but that she was "Not to blame".

An early photograph from 1940, shows a few smartly dressed young women wearing civilian clothes, hats and winter coats, waiting outside the garages. May with her back to the photographer wears a sensible coat and trousers while a colleague models a coat teamed with a fashionable turban. Initially, it was assumed that the photos depicting women wearing smart suits with twin sets and pearls, smart hats and coats, or floral summer dresses were either civilians or off duty. However these were auxiliaries on duty to whom no uniform was issued for the first two years of the war. They are wearing their choice of everyday clothes. In the photo taken in the summer of 1940, Joan Pannell, aged eighteen with her hair stylishly permed, wears a floral summer frock. Marguerite Taylor, wearing blouse and tailored skirt, sits beside Joan on the bumper of a car parked in the garage. A few chose, more sensibly, navy trousers and sweaters but one has to remember that then, trousers for women were not the fashion statement they are today. The ultra smart women wore stylish felt hats, while others sported turbans, both fashionable and a good cover for hair-curlers.

A thin cotton overcoat represented the sole item of uniform issued to ambulance women personnel before 1942 (besides a gaberdine cap with optional ear-flaps). Nick-named the "Flit Coat", it was referred to as such because it reminded the auxiliaries of an advertisement for the pesticide, "Flit". This depicted a man in overalls spraying Flit from a primitive spray gun. Standing by a car, with Station 39 printed on the screen, the photo shows Marguerite Taylor, Shift "B" Leader, wearing the coat and cap, with a steel helmet on her back and the large duty gas mask. Maitt, modelling a woman's "Flit Coat", also poses smirking with one hand delicately on hip while the other holds "his" handbag.

Babette remembers that this was a difficult time because all purchases of clothes had to be accompanied by the requisite numbers of coupons. Allowance of extra coupons was made solely for the purchase of sensible lace-up shoes: nothing being allocated for clothing. She bought a pair of Daks navy trousers and borrowed a white shirt and tie from her brother. The metal auxiliary's badge serves as her tie-pin.

However, when uniforms were issued, a few women paid to have theirs made-to-measure by a tailor. These outfits fitted perfectly, as one would expect. Looking at photographs of May, it is obvious she could not afford such luxuries, nor could most of her companions judging by the ill-fitting, safari-style jackets, skirts or trousers. Mrs Butler, appointed the Station Officer, had a "dress" style uniform bound with violet made up in a very expensive cloth as well as her everyday tailored suit. Enid Dawbarn, as demonstrated in a photograph depicting her greeting wounded troops returning from Africa in 1943, was always perfectly dressed in a tailor-made suit worn with the dress uniform military style cap. She usually wore smart black leather gloves with a cuff, black stockings and her expensive shoes had slight heels. Although all the women could not afford the stylish tailored uniforms, many of them took special care of their appearance. Hair was often carefully permed, make up carefully applied giving an overall appearance of smartness.

The men wore army style "fatigues" in thin navy material which gave them the appearance of a troop of boiler-suited workmen in contrast with the smart females: more practical for working than the women's civilian suits, but hardly stylish as illustrated by the photograph. Of the men, Vernon-Wentworth was always a distinguished looking figure in suit and glasses. The man with pipe in the picture is an officer from the regular ambulance service. One questions the advisability of smoking while servicing a vehicle together with the fact that the fuel store was housed in the garages.

The lack of uniform endured for over two years by the ambulance auxiliaries is in stark contrast with the treatment of volunteers in the Fire Service. Early in the war, Violet Black volunteered for the Auxiliary Fire Service, set up just before the war, while regulars served in the London Fire Brigade. Talking to the press during September 1940, a group of auxiliaries complained that regulars were issued with three changes of uniform while they only had one set. In fact the trousers they received were often not new issue but pressed second-hand pairs. Having been at this incident for the last eighteen hours, they were soaking wet and cold. A colleague had caught pneumonia a few weeks ago and died.

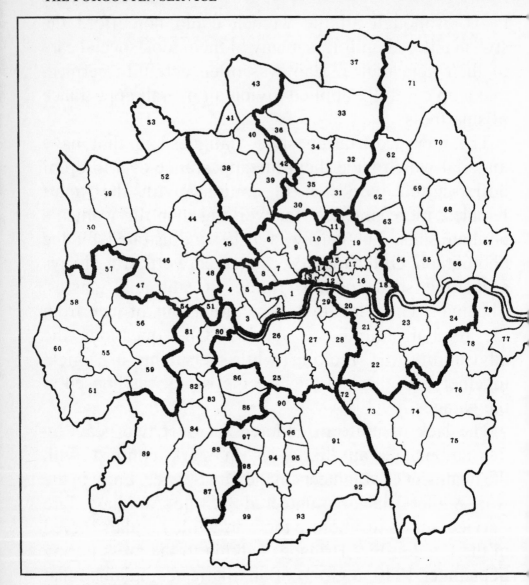

The London Civil Defence Region (No. 5) was divided up into five Groups — Nos. 1, 2 and 3 above the Thames and 4 and 5 below. In addition, four other Groups, Nos. 6-9, covered those areas of Middlesex and Hertfordshire in Greater London. Station 39 lay within Group 2 which covered Hampstead, St Marylebone, Paddington, St Pancras, Islington and Stoke Newington.

MINISTRY OF HOME SECURITY
Composition of Groups in No 5 (London) Civil Defence Region

Group 1: 1 Westminster, **2** Chelsea, **3** Fulham, **4** Hammersmith, **5** Kensington. **Group 2: 6** Hampstead, **7** St Marylebone, **8** Paddington, **9** St Pancras, **10** Islington, **11** Stoke Newington. **Group 3: 12** City of London, **13** Holborn, **14** Finsbury, **15** Shoreditch, **16** Stepney, **17** Bethnal Green, **18** Poplar, **19** Hackney. **Group 4: 20** Bermondsey, **21** Deptford, **22** Lewisham, **23** Woolwich, **24** Greenwich. **Group 5: 25** Wandsworth, **26** Battersea **27** Lambeth, **28** Camberwell, **29** Southwark. **Group 6A: 30** Hornsey, **31** Tottenham, **32** Edmonton **33** Enfield, **34** Southgate, **35** Wood Green, **36** East Barnet, **37** Cheshunt. **Group 6B: 38** Hendon, **39** Finchley, **40** Barnet R.D., **41** Barnet U.D., **42** Friern Barnet, **43** Potters Bar. **Group 6C: 44** Wembley, **45** Willesden, **46** Ealing, **47** Southall, **48** Acton, **49** Ruislip, **50** Uxbridge, **51** Acton, **52** Harrow, **53** Bushey, **54** Brentford & Chiswick. **Group 6D: 55** Feltham, **56** Heston & Isleworth, **57** Hayes & Harlington, **58** Yiewsley & West Drayton, **59** Twickenham, **60** Staines, **61** Sunbury-on-Thames. **Group 7: 62** Walthamstow, **63** Leyton, **64** West Ham, **65** East Ham, **66** Barking, **67** Dagenham, **68** Ilford, **69** Wanstead, **70** Chigwell, **71** Waltham Holy Cross. **Group 8: 72** Penge, **73** Beckenham, **74** Bromley, **75** Orpington, **76** Chislehurst, **77** Crayford, **78** Bexley, **79** Erith. **Group 9A: 80** Barnes, **81** Richmond, **82** Kingston, **83** Malden & Coombe, **84** Surbiton, **85** Merton & Morden, **86** Wimbledon, **87** Ewell, **88** Epsom, **89** Esher. **Group 9B: 90** Mitcham, **91** Croydon, **92** Coulsdon, **93** Purley, **94** Carshalton, **95** Wallington, **96** Beddington, **97** Sutton, **98** Cheam, **99** Banstead.

In May 1941, in the aftermath of one of London's heaviest raids, all the brigades throughout the country were amalgamated into the National Fire Service.

The picture of Babette Loraine and Joan Pannell "modelling" their newly issued uniform suits, dated 1942, is captioned cynically, "My, dear, who is your tailor?" This question sums up an unlikely response to the rest of the women's general appearance. Another photo captioned, "England expects . . ." shows Babette striking a pose. A third pictures a woman standing in an awkward pose showing the ill-fitting uniform at its worst and most hilarious.

All personnel were issued with protective gear which was stored in the ambulance, ready for immediate use. A photo taken early in 1942 shows the regulation wet gear (a set per person was stored in the vehicle) which was to be worn if fire crews were spraying water at the scene of the emergency. In the photograph, Lane, Babette, Wells and Chris Finlay pose self-consciously in front of ambulances. They are enclosed by the all-in-one rubber suits, elasticated at the waist, tin hats with rubber protective covers over the hat and down under the chin leaving only the face visible, (reminiscent of ladies in Regency hats) plus rubber gloves and gum boots. Their large gas masks are in the duffle-type bags slung round their bodies. These Service respirators were of a different style to those issued to the public. Black tin hats were worn by the personnel while white ones, with the rank displayed in black lines, denoted senior officers' ranks. On one occasion the Station Officer gave May an instruction to repaint her helmet white in preparation for a forthcoming parade. Stephanie Currie remembers their helmets were inscribed either "F.A.P." — First Aid Party, or A.A.S. — Auxiliary Ambulance Service. The F.A.P.s were nick-named "Foolish and Pretty".

One volunteer, who had the misfortune to damage his respirator while on duty, was taught a lesson after the regular officers and L.C.C. officials got their heads together. James Cross aged fifty-six, an L.C.C. licensed Public Transport driver who had volunteered for the Service in July 1940, owned his own business. He had offered to work for six days a week without pay. Presumably his wife, Rachel Sybil, would run his pet shop while he was absent. Not only had he a slight knowledge of first aid but had taken an A.R.P. course in anti-gas precautions. In fact the manageress of the A.R.P. canteen, G. S. Armstrong of Gray's Inn, acted as a referee for him saying that she had known him several years and stating, "he would be very capable of the duties required by the Service". His other referee, C. S. Issacs a livestock dealer since 1831 at the Royal Menageries, St Martin's Kennels, W.C.2, confirmed James to be a good driver and thoroughly reliable, practically fearless and in his opinion, "James should be ideal for the job, having been a motorist since 1899".

James sounds just the type of person the Service required, so it is with surprise that one reads of the manner in which he was treated. He wrote to Mr Geach, his station officer at A.A.S. 56, reasonably enough to explain that, while calling at his shop to collect some maps, his Service respirator must have slipped off the passenger seat because he found it on the pavement, damaged beyond repair. This letter, sent to his Station Officer, was forwarded up the chain of command via the Superintendent Ridgwell of South-Eastern Station Ambulance Station, then to the Acting Officer-in-Charge of the London Ambulance Service at Station 6, on to Mr A. G. Hellman, who noted to a Mr Crabb, "I think he should pay to make him more careful in future". The final letter in the file states that "Cross should be required to pay for the replacement of the parts of his civilian duty respirator, damaged due to carelessness on his part at the rates detailed on the form of receipt and undertaking in respect of helmets and respirators".

Personnel who were absent through illness were required to make their excuses by writing to inform their Auxiliary Station Officer. The individual's record card, kept at the local headquarters, showed entries for all absence and unpaid holidays. Rona Crichlow, mentioned earlier, serving at Station 65, was married to a doctor working for the Ministry of Health at Aylesbury. In October 1939 she wrote an informal letter to Mr Matthews at headquarters saying that "I am sorry I was not on duty on Saturday morning — but I had a frightful cold — and thought it better to clear it up before doing night duty."

In December a letter to Mrs Saunders, her Station Officer, explains that she has, "caught cold or something again," she "feels absolutely awful, and that her "bones and head aches" and her throat is "sore". She adds that she feels awful not going on duty when the Station is short-staffed (it was Christmas Eve) and, "maybe will be better by the morning". However when she reported for duty, Miss Bird, noticing Rona had a rash, jumped erroneously to the conclusion that she was suffering from German Measles. Rona, dismissing this claim in a letter to Mrs Saunders dated December 30th, states that she had thought it was something she had caught "from the cat". She mentions that she "managed to see" her husband the day before, adding critically that her husband advised her to "go away for a week or two" but that "a certificate from him will probably not be accepted — I shall send you one from my own doctor later".

Having written a day earlier, from her address at 30 Belsize Park Gardens, to Mr Matthews, the Superintendent at Headquarters, she quotes Miss Bird as having absolutely forbidden her returning to the Station due to the mythical German Measles. She adjudges that Mrs Saunders will have already informed him of that news, which conjures up an annoyed S.O. running along with the gossip. Rona concludes philosophically: "I have thought matters over since I've been away from the Station and come to the conclusion that life there is not conducive to happiness — and I should be glad if you will accept my resignation."

Rona was fortunate to be allowed to resign since on October 22nd, 1940, the L.C.C. Minutes state that "the A.A.S. should be subject to requirements applied to Fire and Rescue Services and should not leave employment without the consent of the officer-in-charge". This resignation was a double loss to the service, having trained Rona for six months as well as the fact that references on file which show her to be a person of quality.

She had given her first referee as a Mr C. A. Betts, the Bank Manager of the Twickenham Branch of the Westminster Bank. He writes to Mr J. Rees, the Superintendent at North-Western Ambulance Station, that Mrs Crichlow has been known to them for sometime. Furthermore they consider her to be, "highly respectable and a quite suitable applicant for the position". Mr Lewis Jones, the headmaster of Georgetown Central School at Tredegar, her second referee, writes: "I have pleasure in attesting to the excellent character and ability of Mrs R. Crichlow who has been personally known to me since some years. She is a person of good education, is eminently practical and is possessed of a very keen intelligence. She is quick to grasp a situation and is quick to react. Her unimpeachable character, lady-like manner and excellent driving capacity should combine to make her a distinct acquisition to the Auxiliary London Ambulance Service."

Alfred John Cross, a fifty-four year old taxi driver, looks on paper to be another ideal choice of volunteer. However he, like Rona Crichlow, left the Service after a few months as his record card bearing the penciled note "dismissal" shows. Alfred had volunteered on September 13th, 1939, at Seven Stars Ambulance Station, listed No. 8. He gave his address as 11 Winslow Road, Fulham, and stated that his preference was to serve in the Fulham area and to train at the Seagrove Road Station. He wrote that he had held a driving licence for thirty-two years and had an L.C.C. licence number 2/496875 (required for a taxi driver) which was valid until May 1940. Two sheets assessing his driving ability are filed. The first test, dated October 9th, 1939, was taken at Seven Stars Ambulance Station and monitored by Superintendent D. Amy. Driving ability was assessed as being "Poor. He is an elderly taxi driver and would want much practice on heavy cars. Seems slightly unbalanced — not safe with an ambulance. Says he has experience but his mechanical knowledge is slight." Amy added that he was able to lift stretchers and, "might make an attendant". Three days later he noted that Cross was "hopeless as a driver, further instruction waste of time. Suggest transferred from Driver to Attendant." A further comment added in a different hand and initialled states: "Remains as a taxi driver to lead convoy."

It is interesting to read Cross took another driving test at 3.30 p.m. on February 9th, 1940, in Bedford Ambulance No. 680 with Superintendent W. F. Snowsie, an examiner at "Headquarters". Although Snowsie writes that his driving ability and physique were good he adds that he "needs medical attention, nerves very bad. Unsafe." A rough draft of a letter initialled by Superintendent Snowsie is filed with Alfred's records:

"Mr Bonner reported that this Aux. had had two driving tests, and was reported to be dangerous on a heavy vehicle. His manner was, also, rather strange, and other auxiliaries at Station had refused to be driven by him. He had been previously at Station 8. Question of transferring him over as an attendant had been considered, but his first aid knowledge was nil, and he was practically a 'passenger' on his station. Aux. tested at H. Q. (Report attached). Afterwards, rang Mr Fawns, and informed him of consequence in dismissal of the aux. Mr Fawns agreed that no mention be made, in letter of termination, of driving criticisms." It would seem reading the note that the Service was unwilling to dismiss Cross because of his poor driving ability — maybe they thought it would be unfair to affect his livelihood. One wonders how his fare paying passengers would feel about their decision!

Fortunately most volunteers rarely caused problems and May records that about half the personnel at Station 39 served with her throughout the duration of the war.

CHAPTER
FOUR

Action Stations

Misses Bruce and Fisher, officers of the L.A.A.S., ran Auxiliary Station 39 until the Blitz struck London. On the night of August 24/25th, 1940, a year after war had been declared, bombs were dropped by a German crew in error on London — a forbidden target. The British War Cabinet immediately responded with an attack by the R.A.F. against Berlin the following night. Tit-for-tat raids by both sides led to Hitler threatening retaliation on a massive scale. On September 7th, a large daylight raid on the East End was followed by a night attack, the bombers being guided by the fires still burning furiously below. That raid killed over 400 Londoners and seriously injured 1,300, yet Misses Bruce and Fisher closed Station 39 and went home. Fortunately few others reacted in the manner of these ladies who had generously offered to return to the Station only on the condition that an air raid shelter was erected for their protection during raids.

I went out the other evening to one of the London Auxiliary Ambulance Service stations, in Greenwich, S.E., and spent the whole night there. We were sitting, eight women and six men, in a sandbagged shelter erected in the playground of an L.C.C. school. Drawn up outside the shelter were seven ambulances, two Green Line coaches and six cars — the station's entire transport fleet.

Since the very first day of the blitz the town has sustained the savage blows of the Luftwaffe, and its A.R.P. workers have been tested as sternly as any in the land. They have passed through the fire — literally so. I met two young men who one night drove an ambulance through a wall of flame to the scene of a bombing.

The strength of this ambulance unit is 68 — 43 women and 25 men. They work in 12-hour shifts, and they are paid the usual A.R.P. rates — £3 3s. 3d. for men and £2.3s. for women. The women include typists, factory workers, housewives and spinsters.

By day the unit occupies the infants' department of a school, the main school building being taken by the A.F.S. At night, as soon as the siren sounds, the men and women on duty take up their quarters in the shelter. And there they sit and wait for the calls that come to them from the district A.R.P. control.

The drivers, men and women alike, go out in rotation, the car drivers alone, the ambulance drivers accompanied by an assistant — out under the splinters and the bombs, to pick up the casualties, take them to the nearest hospital and then return to the station. All the ambulances and the cars already bear the scars of battle — dents and holes made by falling debris or falling splinters. I fancy the unit is secretly proud of them. If the telephone line that connects the district A.R.P. control with the ambulance shelter should break down, the messages are brought by a dispatch rider.

THE WAR ILLUSTRATED, OCTOBER 18th, 1941

R.J. Unstead comments in *Britain in the 20th Century* that "London, which was raided more often than any other city, could 'take it'. . . The courage and tenacity of civilians under attack from the air surprised the British Government which had feared mass hysteria and much heavier casualties culminating in the possibility of the breakdown of the administration."

Typical of the period is the recollection of Mrs Theresa Wilkinson, of 8 Evesham House, Abbey Road, N.W.8 who writes laconically of a night in the Blitz when a bomb rendered her home inhabitable. Dreading what they would find in the lodger's bedroom on the second floor, they made their way upstairs by torchlight:

"On entering and shining a torch, we found the bed piled high with glass and debris. We were afraid for what we might find underneath all that rubble, but we needn't have worried: Mr Robson was still sound asleep, oblivious to all the screeching bombs, heavy gunfire and crashing debris. We decided to leave him in peace: anyone who could sleep like that deserved it."

First out and upon the streets are the stretcher parties, whose work it is to prepare the injured for removal. By the time the ambulances reach the point of impact the casualties are ready for swift examination. It must be decided on the spot whether a casualty must be taken to a hospital or a first aid post. All men and women of the ambulance services are qualified in first aid work. Seventy men and women work constantly in three shifts on the ambulances from this Section, and another 325 people serve on almost the entire range of A.R.P. services. Like the men, an ambulance girl must sign on for duty, and shifts are changed at intervals of about twelve hours. Separate rest rooms are provided for men and women.

Where once goods were stored in almost total darkness is now a well-lighted hive of activity far below street level. Moreover, a series of arches make spacious garages for ambulances, cars and lorries, which can be driven out on to the main London streets at a moment's notice.

ILLUSTRATED, FEBRUARY 1st, 1941

"Later on, after the inevitable cup of tea, everyone went back to bed to try and snatch a little sleep. My slumbers were rudely disturbed by the ringing of the front door bell. I rolled wearily out of bed, only to find myself ankle-deep in icy cold water. When I opened the front door, I found the Rescue Squad waiting on the doorstep and behind them, in the dim light of dawn, I observed a huge crater in the road. They had come to warn everyone that the water and electricity pipes had been badly damaged. We must keep clear of water which might flood the basement. As I had just waded through it the warning was a little late, but presumably the water had not been affected as yet by the electricity.

"The house was by now uninhabitable so everyone had to move out and make other arrangements. I took up a post with the B.B.C. in offices in Oxfordshire, where some of the staff had been evacuated."

May, a Shift Leader, was promoted temporarily to run Station 39. She coped with the demands made on the crews by the added intensity of the day and night raids. She wrote that "a few weeks later a Mrs Butler was posted from Kingston Station. As I had been running the Station she chose me to act as her Deputy Station Officer. The photo shows her wearing one of her expensive tailor-made suits. Mrs Butler was a colourful character who caused me many headaches. I was not solely affected as my colleagues and even some of the L.C.C. officials were involved in this most difficult period at the Station.

"Mrs Butler brought with her six men from her previous station: nicknamed by us as 'her six men'. When off duty, and often when they were all supposed to be on duty, she would socialise with these men. On many occasions she would return with them far too late to meet their duty requirements: they were all paid as full-timers on the Station's personnel. It emerged later that their main occupation was the 'Black Market' though most of them had outside occupations. One was a tic-tac man at the local dog-track and another called himself a dance band leader. To the rest of the ambulance crews they were known as 'Butler's six men'. They were a group apart from the rest of the volunteers and did not mingle, apart from their advances to the women. One of these relationships had tragic consequences resulting in the pregnancy and death of one of the girls. They relied on their influence with Mrs Butler to avoid duties and today would have been called male chauvinists. They expected the girls to wait on them: one would shout for his dinner at the top of his voice. Their presence was an anathema to the middle-class women in our group. It was fortunate that their stay was short-lived.

"Mrs Butler was chauffeured by one of them in a car displaying a doctor's badge — later she appointed Joyce Spencer as her batman to attend her. A doctor's badge enabled the occupant to obtain additional petrol to be used solely for medical emergencies and home visits." May remarked that she never bought any of the Black Market goods offered discreetly by the six men. However, she did mention that food shopping was difficult when working on the short shift in operation at the beginning of the war. Returning home in the early morning would have been an ideal time to queue for the meagre stocks in the shops but she was often too tired. From mid-November, the well-known raid on Coventry marked a change in tactics as the Germans began to concentrate on night attacks. The Luftwaffe carried out raids every night when weather permitted until the devastating incendiary attack on the City of London which took place on the night of December 29/30th. A well-known image captured on film shows the dome of St Paul's emerging above the flames and smoke while London burned. Olive Bargman (née Barnett), an eleven-year-old living with her family at New Cross, about two miles south of the docks on the River Thames, recalls that Sunday night:

"I have the vivid memory of standing outside our air raid shelter at the bottom of the garden. When the raids on London commenced this was to be the night-time refuge where seven of us slept. I was terrified by the sound of the bombers' engines droning overhead. Following the All Clear my father and I, together with our dog Fred, had come out of the shelter to get a breath of air. Looking towards the north the whole sky was red and glowing. Dad said that it looked as though 'the docks had caught it'. Everywhere looked strange and eerie, alight with this strange red glow. Walking down the garden and through the house to the main road, we saw a solid line of fire engines and ambulances making their way towards the river."

Within a few days Olive had been despatched to Wales as an evacuee. A photograph taken a few weeks later shows father and Fred surveying the devastation in their garden where a time-bomb had landed. Olive remembered that her father, having completed a full day's work at the office, would remain there all night on fire duty patrolling the roof tops.

Working by day and being on firefighting duty by night was not the sole prerogative of the "grown-ups". My husband remembers being on a duty rota for fire-watching for one night each week while he was at the grammar school. The sixth form boys were assigned an area to patrol and issued with a bucket and stirrup pump. However by day lessons were not too arduous as all the younger masters had joined up leaving some subjects without staff cover.

Stephanie Currie remembers driving her ambulance from Watford into the City during the Blitz. Stephanie says that "after a particularly heavy raid many buildings in the area around Charing Cross and the station had been demolished, trapping people inside. The R. and D. [Rescue and Demolition] squads were involved in searching for casualties, which we ferried to hospitals, not leaving the scene until all had been rescued. Sally, my attendant, and I had been directed to Trafalgar Square which was the nearest we could drive to the bombed site. Having walked to collect a casualty, we were going back to the ambulance when the blast from a bomb blew me through a shop window. Picking myself up, uninjured, I found my gold watch had gone. It was a square gold shape with a fashionable black material strap, solely of intrinsic value. Funnily enough this upset me greatly."

In common with many of the long-serving personnel May rarely spoke of the gruesome sights; they had already become hardened to survive the constant onslaught on their senses. One incident that she did relate was turned to humour:

"Driving towards Charing Cross with my attendant, we saw the road ahead closed. From a bridge hung a parachute with its land mine still attached underneath, gently swaying in the breeze. All around there was devastation, no living thing moved except for a parrot wandering about amongst the debris, quite bereft of any feathers."

Land mines had a far greater blast effect but obviously could not be dropped accurately. May remembered visiting the Thermionic Club (a London gentlemen's club at No.1 Portland Place) where, following Government advice, the windows had been left slightly open to allow any blast through. Breaking glass was a serious source of injuries, even though windows had been criss-crossed with tape. May remembers that "we walked into the club lounge to be met with the grisly sight of several headless gentlemen sitting in armchairs, their heads having been blown off by the blast of the bomb coming through the window."

A trawl through the message slips recording telephone calls between Control, Wardens, Ambulance, Fire and Police revealed that on the night of December 8/9th, 1940, the club had been "previously damaged by a land mine. Some electric cables fused, slight fire. Incident 426."

The mayhem had been caused when a land mine exploded opposite the B.B.C. in Portland Place. Initially a Warden on the roof of the building reported to Control at St Marylebone Ambulance Station that he could see the parachute slowly descending. Station 39 was requested to send an ambulance and by chance this was driven by Joan Davies. Her husband, Ivor Walsworth, worked for the B.B.C, which meant that Joan was well-known to Police Constable John Vaughan, the regular officer on duty at the entrance. He gave her a cheery welcome and enquired why she had brought her ambulance, but within a few minutes he was dead, beheaded by the blast as the mine exploded.

Another terse message about Incident 426, timed at 23.09, stated that a high explosive bomb has blown up. By 23.15 it was estimated that there would be at least fifty casualties as well as a fire hazard. Throughout the night, Control deployed ambulances from Station 39, a few hundred yards away, with back up sent from Station 37 in Edgware Road. Until the emergency was under control, personnel were expected to forego their official shift's end and work on. Babette remembers only one woman who refused to so do.

Mrs Byrne was employed as a cook at Broadcasting House; she later related her fearsome account of this night to her lodger, Mrs Theresa Wilkinson:

"As I left the building after a session in the canteen, I passed the time of day with P. C. Vaughan who was on duty. Realising I had left my gloves in the cloakroom, I returned in the lift to the lower ground floor. It was at this moment that the bomb fell and the policeman, with whom I had just spoken, was killed. I felt completely stunned at the terrible suddenness with which life can be ended."

By 02.10 a message from Hill Street Mortuary informed Control that "one body, male, policeman from Incident 426 has been received". In the early morning they reported an unidentified body died on the way to the mortuary. Due to the water main and sewers bursting, ambulances had to be sent to Matron's Room at Broadcasting House to remove the injured. A Fire Officer employed by the B.B.C. reported the following observations concerning Incident 426 to Colonel Stone at Marylebone Borough A.R.P, Marylebone Town Hall:

December 12th, 1940

"Dear Colonel Stone,
"At 10.55 pm. on the night of December 8th, a land mine exploded at Portland Place, opposite the west end of Broadcasting House. The parachute was actually seen by the Defence Officer on the roof, who was able to report the fact by telephone before the explosion took place.

"As a result of the explosion practically all the offices on the west side of Broadcasting House were wrecked, though the damage to the offices on the 5th, 6th and 7th floors were confined to broken windows and fittings. The offices on the east side of the building were only affected by blast to a minor degree and comparatively few windows were broken. The offices on the south side of the building and some on the north were rather more seriously affected. A number of fires followed the explosion. Most of these were extinguished by our fire squads, but that on the 3rd floor became serious and extended to one of the studios inside the tower. It was finally extinguished by the Fire Brigade. As the fire penetrated one of the ventilation ducts some difficulty was experienced in putting this out. There was some flooding of the basement and sub-basement, due to the water used by the Fire Brigade. This, of course, was unavoidable.

"The cause of the fires is unknown. It may have been fusing of wires, but I think, on the whole, it is more likely it was from the explosion itself which set fire to the scaffolding on the west side of the building, the flames from which penetrated inside the building. Casualties treated: —

B.B.C. Staff: 4 to hospital, 5 First Aid treatment.

Police: 1 killed 2 to hospital.

Military: 5 First Aid treatment.

Outsiders: 4 to hospital.

'The following information as to the nature of the parachute may be of interest.

"1. Defence Officer on the roof says that the parachute was dark in colour and appeared to extend almost across Portland Place, the whole span probably being about 60 feet.

"2. Another member of the staff, who was with the policeman on point duty opposite Broadcasting House, actually saw the parachute descending. He reports that the parachute was open at the top and looked rather like a handkerchief with 15-20 foot ropes. Three or four explosions seemed to occur a fraction of a second after each other. This man, whose name is MacGregor, was lucky to escape with his life.

> Yours faithfully,
> R. S. Stafford."

On the night of December 8th, I left the B.B.C. shortly after 10.45 and accompanied by a colleague, Mr Sibbick, went to the cycle shed in Chapel Mews. The customary nightly air raid was in progress and, as we left the cycle shed, we could hear the distant sound of aircraft and A.A. gun-fire. We were just entering Hallam Street from the Mews when I heard a shrieking, whistling noise like a large bomb falling. This noise continued for about three seconds and then abruptly ceased as if in mid-air. There was no thud, explosion or vibration. (I particularly remember this as I had heard this happen once before, and was curious as to what caused it and why it stopped.)

Then came the sound of something clattering down the roof of a building in the direction of Broadcasting House. I looked up thinking that it might be incendiaries but this was not so. We slowly walked round to the entrance to Broadcasting House and estimate that we took about three and a half minutes in doing so. My colleague went inside, returned the cycle shed key and cycled off towards Oxford Circus.

I remained outside the entrance talking to two policemen and enquiring about possible diversions on my route home. They were P.C.s Vaughan and Clarke. A saloon car was parked alongside the kerb, some distance round from the entrance, and I could see to the left of the car the lamp post in the middle of the road opposite the Langham Hotel. The policemen had their backs to this and so did not observe what followed.

Whilst we were conversing I noticed a large, dark, shiny object approach the lamp post and then recede. I concluded that it was a taxi parking. It made no noise. The night was clear with only a few small clouds: there was moonlight from a westerly direction, but Portland Place was mainly in shadow. All three of us were wearing our steel helmets. (My chin strap was round the back of my head, and I had been advised to wear it so, shortly after I was issued with the helmet.) A few seconds later, I saw what seemed to be a very large tarpaulin of a drab, or khaki, colour fall in the same spot. The highest part of it was about ten or twelve feet above the road when I first saw it and it seemed to be about twenty-five feet across. It fell at about the speed of a pocket handkerchief when dropped and made no noise. Repair work was being carried out on Broadcasting House and I, not unnaturally, concluded that it was a tarpaulin which had became detached and fallen from the building into the roadway. There were no outside warnings of any imminent danger.

I drew the attention of the policemen to it, they turned round and could see nothing. It had collapsed and from where we were was partly screened by the car, and the roadway at that point was in shadow. They told me that they could not see anything and then followed some banter, but I persisted in saying that I had seen something fall in the road. They then decided to go to investigate. A third P.C., Mortimer, had meanwhile approached us. He was about to conduct a lady across that part of the road. But after hearing that I had seen something, he told me that he was taking her inside the building while they found out what it was.

P.C. Vaughan drew ahead of P.C. Clarke who stopped at the kerb to ask me just exactly where it had dropped. I went over towards him calling out that I would show him it. It was about a minute since I had seen the "dark object'. I went towards the "tarpaulin" and had reached a spot to the left of Clarke, about six feet from the kerb and twenty-five to thirty feet from the "thing" when P.C. Vaughan came running towards me at high speed. He shouted something which I did not hear properly for at that moment my attention was drawn to a very loud swishing noise as if a plane were diving with engine cut off, or like a giant fuse burning. It lasted 3 to 4 seconds. It did not come from the lamp post end of the "thing" but it may have come from the other end.

P.C. Vaughan passed me on my left and P.C. Clarke, who apparently had understood the shout, also ran towards the building. Realising that I would have to turn "right about" before I could start running, I crouched down in what is known as "Prone Falling Position No. 1". Even at that moment I did not imagine that there was any danger in the road and thought it was coming from above, in Portland Place. My head was up, watching, and, before I could reach "Position No.2", and lie down flat, the "thing" in the road exploded. I had a momentary glimpse of a large ball of blinding white light with two concentric rings of colour, the inner one lavender and outer one violet, as I ducked my head. (The "ball" seemed to be about ten to twenty feet high, and was near the lamp post.) Several things happened simultaneously, my head was jerked back due to a heavy blow on the dome and rim of the back of my steel helmet. I do not remember this for as my head went back, I received a severe blow on my forehead and at the bridge of my nose. The blast bent up the front rim of my steel helmet and knocked it off my head. The explosion made an indescribable noise, something like a colossal growl, and was accompanied by a veritable tornado of air blast. I felt an excruciating pain in my ears and all sounds were replaced by a very loud singing noise, (which I was told later was when I lost my hearing and had my eardrums perforated.) I felt that consciousness was slipping from me and at that moment I "heard" a clear loud voice shouting, "Don't let yourself go! Face up to it and hold on." It rallied me and, summoning all my will power and energy, I succeeded in forcing myself down into a crouching position with my knees on the ground, my feet against the kerb behind me and my hands covering my face. I remember having to move them over my ears because of the pain in them, doubtless due to the blast. It seemed to ease the pain.

Then I received another hit on the forehead and felt weaker. The blast seemed to have come in successive waves accompanied by vibrations from the ground. I felt as if it were trying to "spin" me and tear me away from the kerb. Then I received a very heavy blow just in front of the right temple, which knocked me down on my left side in the gutter. (Later in the First Aid Post, they removed what they described as a "piece of bomb" from that wound.) Whilst in the gutter, I clung on to the kerb with both hands and with my feet against it. I was again hit in the right chest (and later found that my double-breasted overcoat, my coat, leather comb case and papers had been cut through and a watch in the top right-hand pocket of my waistcoat had the back dented in and its works broken).

Just as I felt that I could not hold out much longer I realised that the blast pressure was decreasing and a shower of dust, dirt and rubble swept across me. Pieces penetrated my face, some skin was blown off, and something pierced my left thumb-nail and my knuckles were cut, causing me involuntarily to let go my hold on the kerb. Instantly, although the blast was dying down, I felt myself being slowly blown across the pavement towards the wall of the building. I tried to hold on, but there was nothing to hold on to. Twice I tried to rise, but seemed held down; eventually I staggered to my feet. I looked around, and it seemed like a scene from Dante's Inferno. The front of the building was lit by a reddish-yellow light, the saloon car was on fire to the left of me and the flames from it were stretching out towards the building and not upwards. Pieces of brick, masonry and glass seemed to appear on the pavement, making, to me, no sound. A few dark huddled bodies were round about and right in front of me were two soldiers, one, some feet from a breach in the wall of the building, where a fire seemed to be raging, was propped up against the wall with his arms dangling by him, like a rag doll. The other was nearer, about twelve feet from the burning car. He was sitting up with his knees drawn up and supporting himself by his arms. His trousers had been blown off him. I could see that his legs were bare and that he was wearing short grey underpants. He appeared to be shouting for assistance.

I made for the entrance of the building to get help. It was obscured by dust, smoke and fumes and I nearly fell over a large steel plate which had fallen down and was blocking the entrance. I shouted for help several times, and then realised that no one could get out until the obstruction had been removed. Fearing that the car's tank would explode and envelope the injured soldier in flames, I hurried back to him, and with him clinging to me, we were able to reach the entrance where he sat down as entry was still blocked. I told him to hang on to an upright at the entrance and to shout like hell for assistance should he see or hear anyone approaching. I went back to look at the other soldier. He was still in the same posture and I feared that he was dead. I looked around: there was a long dark body lying prone, face downwards, close to the kerb in front of the building. It may have been P.C. Vaughan. There appeared to be one or two dark huddled bodies by the wall of the building. I had not the strength to lift any of them.

I wondered where the water was coming from, which I felt dripping down my face, and soon discovered that it was blood from my head wounds. I could see no one moving anywhere and, until the entrance was clear, I thought I would look round for my steel helmet and gas mask, which I had slung round me at the time of the explosion. I soon found the gas mask and picked up a steel helmet which was not mine.

I was then joined by my colleague, who had returned, and went with him to the entrance where I shouted for assistance for those outside and for someone to bring firefighting appliances to put out the car fire as I was afraid the glare would invite further missiles or destruction.

I walked down to our First Aid Post, where I was treated, and then to Listening Hall 1 where I rested until I was taken away by stretcher party and sent to the Middlesex Hospital. Here I received every possible attention and kindness.

Later on I was told that the "thing" had been a land mine and that its explosion or blast had lasted for nine seconds.

The effect of the blast on my clothes is possibly of interest. I was wearing bicycle clips round the bottoms of my trousers at the time. After the blast was over, my double-breasted overcoat was slit up to the back and torn in several places, but was being held together by the belt. My trousers and underpants were pitted with small cuts about an inch long but presumably the bicycle clips prevented the draught getting up my trousers and tearing them off. A woollen scarf knotted round my neck undoubtedly saved my neck and chest from small fragments, such as were removed from my face, which was not covered by my scarf.

L. D. MacGregor

Engineer, Technical Recording Section
British Broadcasting Corporation.
March 7th, 1941.

It was mandatory for any building employing thirty people or more to have fire-wardens at roof-top level twenty-four hours a day. In fact an official press release a few days later, states that on the terrible night of December 29/30th, 1940, many fires took hold because fire-watchers were not in place.

This incident was just one of several involving Station 39 each night. On October 15th, for example, two months before the mine dropped opposite Broadcasting House, a delayed-action bomb had scored a direct hit on the B.B.C. Logged as Incident 303, at 21.00 a soldier sent by the Warden at Post D5 reported that the heavy explosive bomb had caused a fire on the fifth floor. Within six minutes, ambulances were requested by Control from Station 39. By 21.16 a worried Warden on the roof of Orchard Court reported two lights showing from the building. He was given the answer that Broadcasting House was on fire. The Fire Brigade was alerted and the area evacuated. At 21.54 a message stated: "Stretcher party trapped on Floor 3. Fire on Floor 5. Beware debris". Throughout the next two days rescue teams searched for bodies: twelve had been recovered to date which, together with a leg found on the fifth floor, were taken to Paddington Mortuary. Sections of the structure were in danger of movement and the Borough Engineer was instructed to send "jacks, poles and lamps etc". Many were trapped in the debris and the Warden in charge would call out for absolute quiet listening for any sounds beneath the rubble while a tracker dog systematically covered the area. This scenario was a well-practised routine and had been so for months.

Stephanie Currie recalls being involved in a rescue underneath tons of debris. Driving back to Watford from a call-out into London, she was stopped by an air raid warden at Highbury Corner. As she climbed down from the cab, she related how the warden remarked, "'You're thin enough,' as he led us to a bombed house. Tersely he explained that two infants were trapped underneath the rubble. As he spoke the house emitted a groan and settled onto the upended timbers. He said that he thought there would be sufficient space for me to squeeze through the tunnel and into the bedroom where the children were entombed. I crawled through and came out under the baby's cot. Rescuing her, I wrapped her in blankets for protection as I tried to persuade the older child to creep towards me through a small space. Feeling the horror of claustrophobia for the first time, I saw a toy train amongst the debris. Whispering to the little boy that we were playing trains, I told him to grab my ankles. Puff, puffing we went down the tunnel, slowly emerging into daylight. Having checked the children and found them sound, the A.R.P. ferried them to the Metropolitan Hospital and we continued on our way home to Watford. Sadly I did not ask the children's names: maybe they were not known."

Most ambulance service personnel carried out their duties unrecorded. Jean Bowden writing in *Call an Ambulance* published in 1963 states that only three Ambulance Silver Medals had been awarded since inception in 1938. Awarded for meritorious conduct, it is surprising that the first presentation was not made until 1952. It is interesting to read in the records at Westminster that awards mentioned in the minutes for one month in 1941 state that the National Fire Service had received 46 medals, the Rescue Services 18 and the Ambulance Service, both Regular and Auxiliary, a mere 2 medals. This was typical yet the reason cannot have been a lack of courage. However the London Gazette for May 30th, 1941, lists the award of the British Empire Medal (Civil) to six members of the London Auxiliary Ambulance Service (see page 183).

May remembers the interest caused at the Station by the publication of intriguing news about their senior officer: "On November 3rd, 1941, The *Evening News* printed a startling story stating that Mrs Butler was in fact a titled Lady. The newspaper had made the link with the ambulance service because Lady Josephine, the President of the London Amateur Boxing Club, was selling tickets for a Boxing Tournament from 25-42 Weymouth Mews, the address of our Station 39. Interviewed by a reporter, Mrs Butler (alias Lady Josephine) remarked that she had kept her secret for the last forty years, promising her family that she would never use her title. Even now she said she would keep her father's name a secret. In fact, as Mrs Butler told the *Evening News* reporter: "You will not find anything about me in any reference books of titled persons: that's because I prefer to be known at the moment as Mrs Butler. My marriage to Mr Butler was secret, and I am not going to tell you where it took place.

"I am chairman of the Ambulance Benevolent Fund and the fact that my title appears on the official notepaper is because the Fund has to register and it is essential that I should give my correct name. I know many people who would like to know the name of the Earl, but that's my secret."

Babette Loraine recalls vividly the day the Press arrived at the Station to interview "Lady Josephine".

"The Press arrived at the Station on November 1st, 1941, to request a photograph of Lady Josephine. We were intrigued by the story. 'Lady Josephine' insisting that she must be photographed with some of her staff, chose Joan Pannell and myself, I expect because we were the two of the younger members. However for later photo calls, Mrs Butler preferred to be pictured alone."

May recalls that "a few evenings later, Finlay being on patrol duty, halted a Rolls-Royce as it glided towards the Station. Lady Josephine, dressed in a smartly tailored grey dress-uniform braided with cerise (she was attending a social function), called out that it was her father's car and that the crates of champagne in the boot were from his cellars. Typically she had overlooked the name of Barkers Stores printed on the outside. Lady Josephine was on her way, she stated, 'to inspect an Italian prisoner of war camp in order to sort them out because they are all homosexuals'".

Christina Finlay, recounting this episode to her friends, told how she had seen the name of the hire company fixed to the rear bumper of the Rolls. "Mrs Butler became very friendly with Joyce Spencer, whose father was a well-known figure in the medical profession. Spencer acted as her batman, driving her and running errands. It is interesting to note that although

Mrs Butler claimed to be both a driver and a pilot, we knew that she was unable to drive. On one occasion I heard her instruct Spencer to take 'her' car to a garage in Portland Street and sell it. Spencer duly returned with the cash. I established that the car was not hers to sell.

"Due to my promotion to Deputy Station Officer I had responsibility for various administrative duties. Working in the office I became concerned that the numerous cheques that arrived for the newly-formed Ambulance Benevolent Fund, whose registered address was given as Station 39, were not paid into a named account for the fund. Mrs Butler instructed me to take cheques to her bank and pay them directly into her personal account. On numerous occasions I queried the wisdom of doing this and suggested another special named account solely for the fund. Mrs Butler replied that she would continue to have the money paid into her personal account, adding, 'They can have the money when they ask!'"

"The apparent ease with which I observed Lady Josephine forging the signatures of my colleagues, marking people present who in fact were absent, caused me further concern. Despite the ethics of so doing, it meant that the Station was often seriously understaffed in fact but not, of course, on paper. While nominally on duty, Mrs Butler and her six men left the Station 39 to frequent night clubs, boxing matches and similar venues in the evenings and often through the night. Asking the advice of my father, a retired Police Inspector, he warned me to be careful not to become implicated in what was taking place. However I became seriously worried daily lest my signature be forged. When I was ordered to sign for some new tyres which I had not seen arrive, I refused.

"On another occasion Mrs Butler asked me who had a typewriter. Replying that Loraine, who was learning to type in her spare time, had one, she duly borrowed it. Pulling notes from her bag, Mrs Butler settled down to type letters in the office. While typing she looked up and asked me if I knew the exact address of the Bath Club in Jermyn Street. My suspicions were fully aroused by now because of many other incidents which had left me greatly concerned. Observing her discarding crumpled sheets to the wastepaper basket, I retrieved several copies which I concealed in my civilian respirator box. Handing me a sealed letter to post (it was 2 a.m), she said: 'Go home, Greenup. It's a quiet night,' and adding, 'Drop this letter in the post'".

"These discarded letters purported to come from the Bath Club and were signed by 'Lord Winterton'. His 'Lordship' begged the addressee to support, with a generous donation to Lady Josephine, the secret force which was being formed, 'behind enemy lines to prepare for the invasion'. Any appeal so worded at a time when Britain was in serious danger would have touched every heart. In view of the events, unknown to us that were taking place in Mrs Butler's personal life, I had every reason 'to watch my back'."

Babette remembers her typewriter well as "my mother and I had shared the cost of buying it as we were both in the process of learning the skills. Mrs Butler did not return the machine stating that it must have been stolen from the Station. I said that I would inform the local police station but she told me not to bother them as she had 'friends at Scotland Yard'. Calling into the local station weeks later, I found they had no record of my loss. Months later a formal enquiry was held by officers who descended suddenly on the Station to enquire into the difficulties and discrepancies experienced by staff while serving under Mrs Butler. All personnel were invited to attend individually to air their grievances. Having mentioned my missing typewriter I was instructed to appear before the officers. On entering the room, I saw Mrs Butler sitting at the side of their table. During the time in which I explained my loss, Mrs Butler never spoke a word. I never saw my typewriter again."

May continues her story by describing the incidents that led up to the official investigation:

"One day Mrs Butler informed me that she and her 'six men' were going to a boxing match at the hall in Seymour Road Baths instead of manning the Station. I did not mark the seven present, as she had instructed, but left the spaces blank on purpose. Being severely understaffed as a result of her actions, I telephoned Headquarters to request reinforcements to augment my staff. No comment was made but an officer went to the boxing match and found the men gone. The next day a visiting officer, making a random check, queried this error to which the 'Lady' replied as follows, no doubt believing it to be true: 'My deputy is as thick as a plank'.

"An investigation of Mrs Butler followed headed by a K.C. and a team including L.C.C. officials. They found, hidden in a cupboard, hundreds of stubs representing tickets for charity she had sold on behalf of the Amateur Boxing Association: but not the cash. She was summarily suspended and the six men dispersed, possibly to other stations. However the next day I received a telephone call from her to request that I have her helmet painted white for the parade she had been going to head the following day. (Officers wore white helmets to distinguish them from the ranks.) As her suspension had been given as 'sick leave', she was able to return to her duties with impunity but on the understanding that she was not allowed to touch any accounts or book-keeping.

"A few weeks later she was ordered to attend at County Hall with all her books and receipts. She was never seen again at the Station. Later I discovered from the report of her trial, in connection with a different matter featured in the *Evening Standard,* that she had been given a job as clerk earning £3. 3. 6d a week. It is interesting to note that the salary of Station Officer for a seventy-two hour week was £3. 18. 9d.

"Today", said May, "these wild tales may seem amusing but in wartime when morale needed to be high her actions and lack of leadership had thoroughly demoralised Station 39. It was into this scenario that I was designated the Acting Station Officer on June 7th, 1942, replacing Mrs Butler and having full responsibility for the staff of eighty. The immediate result of her leadership was apparent in the poor morale of the Station which I set about improving. My rank as Station Officer being confirmed on August 13th, I held this position until we were disbanded in 1945. Enid Dawbarn, the daughter of the owner of the Fine Arts Society in Bond Street, was appointed as my Deputy.

"Later I heard from an L.C.C. official that Mrs Butler's reinstatement was due solely to the fact that she had a friendship with a high-ranking official and his wife who was also an Auxiliary Ambulance Station Officer. My source explaining the facts, thanked me for my part in unmasking the deceptions and remarked that many heads would have rolled in the event of further delay. In fact he believed that his job had been in jeopardy as she had been showering him with gifts. However the full repercussions of these events were suppressed at a high level.

"Discipline and morale being at a low point, I decided to set out the daily and weekly tasks to be undertaken by the shifts. This I presented in clear and concise form. Enid Simon, who was learning the skills, typed the sheets for me."

These sheets remain intact today despite having been typed on the wartime "flimsy" paper which was used by all local government departments at that time. The first section outlines the duties to be undertaken on a twenty-four hour shift. The second section gives a more general outline of the weekly duties. The final section details the extra duties undertaken to assist the war effort. May wrote these programmes in preparation before issuing standing orders (in the style reminiscent of a teacher). Written in 1942, it is reproduced opposite unaltered in its entirety:

During the dense fog on 11th-12th, November, 1942, heavy calls were made on the London Ambulance Service. A total of 200 accident calls and 267 general calls was dealt with on 11th November, 1942, of which 96 accident calls and 21 general calls were received between 6p.m. and midnight. The accident calls for the whole day were twice, and those for the evening three times, the normal number. Owing to this large number of calls and the length of time taken to reach the scene of many of the accidents, the regular fleet of vehicles proved insufficient during the evening, and the Auxiliary Ambulances normally reserved for air raid casualties, were brought into use. The regular Service are now staffed partly by men and partly by women, while the Auxiliary Service is staffed mainly by women.

The density of the fog made it necessary to arrange many of the Ambulance crews so that one or more members of a crew could act as guides. All the staff responded with success to the heavy demands made on them, and the work was undertaken in an excellent spirit, and in no case was there any failure of an Ambulance to reach the scene of an accident, though there was, of course, much delay.

Journeys took a long time to complete. Most vehicles had to be guided by a member of the crew walking in front and illuminating the kerb or the white line in the middle of the road. One Ambulance progressed up a main thoroughfare under the guidance of nine men and women with torches: their trip of $1^3/_4$ miles took 1 hour and 10 minutes.

The tasks undertaken included the conveyance of a large number of victims of accidents due to the fog, maternity patients (the crew of one vehicle gave valuable help to a doctor in charge of a maternity patient), domiciliary midwifes, and infectious and other sick persons. A party of elderly male patients from a country hospital travelling to a London hospital was delayed for four or five hours and had to be fed, tended and cheered in one of the Ambulance Stations.

Ambulances were called to many places not easy to find even in normal conditions; some accidents were on railway lines, in docks and other remote parts, making the task of location and transport even more difficult. The Service as a whole continued to function as expeditiously as the exceptionally difficult weather conditions permitted, and particular credit is due to the crews of the Auxiliary vehicles who undertook unusual duties under specially onerous conditions. They showed tenacity and resourcefulness in coping with the varied problems which faced them. The normal Headquarters staff attending the Ambulance switchboard, reinforced by volunteers, worked under great pressure in dealing with the many calls received and in solving the innumerable problems which confronted them.

An expression of appreciation of their resourcefulness and devotion to duty has been conveyed to the staff concerned.

SOMERVILLE HASTINGS, CHAIRMAN,
COUNTY HALL MINUTES, DECEMBER 1st, 1942

PROGRAMME OF WORK AT STATION 39

DAILY PROGRAMME

09.00 Change of shift. This is a time often busy for the storekeeper who sees numbers of the opposite shift; also for Canteen managers who exchange ideas and pass over keys, cash-boxes, books etc. Members of oncoming shift sign a time table for the short leave they would like. The whole of the premises are inspected by the two shift leaders and any auxiliaries who have done work badly are called back to complete it to the satisfaction of the oncoming shift leader.

09.00-9.30 A time used for settling in and changing into working clothes while shift leaders report the state of parties and fill up manning board. They also give out previously prepared orderly lists and make a patrol list for the day, to fit in with the various duties, short leaves, vocational classes etc. Special instructions or orders for the day are written on the blackboard with times of lectures or practices for the shift to see. Mess managers use this time to give out stores to the cook.

09.30 Cleaning materials given out by a storekeeper.

09.30-10.30 Every vehicle is checked and cleaned — with shortage of staff this often means that one team has to do two ambulances or cars. The driver fills up a rough log book, records mileage, lights, petrol, water and oil.

From these the shift leader fills in the regulation log books. The team of each ambulance work together but usually the driver is the one to clean the engine and polish the bonnet and wings, also cabin, while the attendant washes the inside of the ambulance and checks the fittings. The whole, inside and out, is cleaned every day, but special attention is paid to some particular part on different days of the week — see weekly routine. In rotation the blankets of each ambulance are aired and changed. (No.1 Ambulance on Monday and No. 2 on Tuesday etc.)

10.30. Patrol duties commence in garages and continue at hourly stretches throughout the day until 23.00. The coal and coke ration is issued by the appointed person on each shift — collected by the sitting room orderly for the women's quarters and by one of the men for the men's room. Then follows a break for refreshment and the canteen and dining room orderlies begin their long day of meal serving and clearing and washing up.

11.00 Work is resumed — either extra cleaning of vehicles or premises. A. R. P. practices or lectures. The learner drivers may go out for practice drives while the canteen manager goes out to the shops, either on foot or cycle. As no shops deliver nowadays her task is not a light one and another auxiliary sometimes accompanies the mess manager.

13.00 Lunch prepared by cook but served and washed up by the two canteen orderlies and the dining room orderly afterwards clears the tables and sweeps the floor.

13.30. Fire lit in common sitting room by sitting room orderly. The afternoon is the most popular time for short leave. Those who are left on duty may do any small extra tasks, such as cleaning windows, mending black-out curtains, touching up paint on vehicles or washing tea cloths, dusters, cleaning rags and cushion covers.

16.30. Tea prepared and served by canteen orderlies. Hurricane lamps are then filled and lit. Any shutters which still work are pulled down. All black-out is done and inspected by patrol at the time. Lights on vehicles are checked either by A. S. O. or D. A. S. O. [Ambulance Station Officer or Deputy], or shift leader and one auxiliary. As the cook leaves at 16.00 hours the preparation of supper is carried on by the canteen orderlies. There may be some Table Tennis. During the evening there will probably be black-out driving practice for three of the personnel, who have a list of places to visit, such as Hospitals, A. R. P. Warden's Posts, Rest Centres, Mortuary etc . . .

20.00. Supper — followed by washing up and tidying the dining room again.

20.30. Practically every evening there is a practice message communications exercise which keeps a telephonist busy for an hour and recently, when there has been no such exercise, there have been parties of wardens wishing to have stretcher loading demonstrated to them. After supper everyone not otherwise engaged generally sits in the common room when needlework and knitting are brought out. It is a useful time for any informal discussion — two or three may play Table Tennis.

23.00-07.00 The fire picket of four takes over patrol and telephone duties. The first outside picket inspects all firefighting equipment. This party usually includes one part-time auxiliary.

07.00 The office orderly relieves the telephonist and scrubs and dusts the office.

07.30 Breakfast — followed by washing up and tidying the kitchen for canteen orderlies.

08.00 Shift leader relieves office orderly. Between 08.00 and 09.00 the whole of the flat, six rooms, two bathrooms and staircases and the games room are swept, dusted and mopped by the rest of the shift who are each responsible for one department. Fires are cleared out, ashes sieved and all salvage and pig food removed to appropriate bins. Hurricane lamps are put away and shutters pulled up. All beds are aired and turned back and bedding put away.

The strength of this programme that May drafted lies in its pedantic attention to detail. There would be shifts when no emergency occurred therefore it was vital to ensure that crews were kept busy for much of the day. Before the alternate shift took over, the incoming and outgoing shift leaders inspected the work completed and a signature was required before takeover was complete. No signature would be given until the shift leader was convinced all was correct, in fact any individual with whom fault was found had to remain until the officer was finally satisfied.

Reference is made to the salvage and pig food in the final paragraph. Every scrap of rejected food scraped from plates together with potato peelings, cabbage leaves and kitchen detritus was collected in large dustbins for making into swill for pigs. During the war everyone was encouraged to collect such "waste". The author's family kept a few hens as eggs were in short supply. I can still smell the aroma of that swill being boiled up in a large saucepan on the kitchen stove. During the 1914-1918 war, a relative's farm in Suffolk suffered a devastating foot and mouth attack due, it was proved, to the swill delivered from the Italian P.O.W. camp in the village. No portion of pork should be put in the pigs' waste lest an incipient virus be transmitted to livestock.

The weekly programme written by May as a guide to remind her of work in hand was as follows:

WEEKLY PROGRAMME

MONDAY. Special attention is given to everything concerning the wheels and tyres of all vehicles. Tyres are pumped up to correct pressure, wheels specially cleaned and the driver ensures that all nuts on wheels are moveable. Under wings and under-carriage also receive attention. Two auxiliaries may be appointed to collect dirty laundry from about nine stations in the area, deliver it at Lawn Road [the area Headquarters] and then issue the clean laundry to the same stations.

TUESDAY. All batteries are inspected, topped up with distilled water if necessary and lugs treated with Vaseline. A special check is taken of the tools on each vehicle. Drivers' cabins are cleaned thoroughly, also the underside of bonnets. At 11.00 there is a stretcher drill for all on duty. On Tuesdays the A. S. O. or D. A. S. O., whichever is on duty, prepares the pay sheets and staff and sick returns. At 14.00 there is now marching practice. The mess manager tidies cupboards and prepares the order for the L. C. C. food stores.

WEDNESDAY. All ambulance roofs mopped, outside of body polished with furniture polish and all white paint is washed and gumptioned if necessary. Buckles on straps are polished and stretcher runners treated with furniture polish. At 11.00 there is stirrup pump drill for all and maybe a reminder about the disposal of firefighting equipment or position of main taps. The pay sheets are completed ready for collection or our station may be the one chosen to do the collecting (which is from eight or ten stations) for delivery to the M. W. Pay Office. The mess manager pays all weekly bills and finishes off the accounts for the week.

* * *

THURSDAY. First aid lecture from 10.00 — 12.00 so no extra cleaning is done. The storekeeper collects stores from M. W. A. S. on alternate Thursdays. This is the day when she does up the books and after putting stores away tidies the cupboards and cleans out the storerooms. The pay men arrive in the morning and after their visit National Savings are collected.

FRIDAY. National Savings collected from opposite shift. At 11.00 Respirator drill followed by wearing and cleaning. The canteen manager collects stores from Worrington Road Schools and when putting them away tidies the cupboards and brings the stock book up-to-date. 16.15 A. R. P. lecture.

SATURDAY. This morning is devoted to a special cleaning up of all garage premises and the shelter. They are all swept, disinfected and swilled as much as the water shortage permits. Windows are also cleaned. The canteen orderlies do all the cooking as this is the cook's rest day.

Water shortages were often experienced when mains were severed by bombing and mention is made of cleaning the garages and air raid shelter with as much water as the shortage permits. During the war, even filling a bath at home was restricted to a depth of four inches. One personal memory of the author is of the next-door neighbour, who was also the warden for the road, calling with a pamphlet which stated that the bath level must be restricted to four inches. Putting a couple of inches of water into the bath led to tears and misery until mother came with an assurance that the level was lower than necessary. Throughout the war, the population, albeit ever so young, devoutly followed the most "nannyish" of rules and regulations.

May preserved a poem (reproduced overleaf) entitled *Lines to a Young Man* handwritten by Alan Braley, which portrays a light-hearted version of the routine while extolling the virtues of Station 39. The verse is execrable and the sentiments expressed at odds with the facts, however the allusions to staff make it of interest. Alan Braley was one of two conscientious objectors who joined from another Station where they were being victimised. He comments that serving at Station 39 is preferable to "going down a mine", an option offered to conscientious objectors. Although the poetic value may be low, the sentiments give a tongue in cheek comment on the manner in which the sexes had equal opportunities. After Mrs Butler and her "six men" left, male chauvinism was neither appreciated nor allowed.

Every statement made in the poem is the antitheses of life on the Station. Alan mentions that Lane, Chris Finlay or Babette would do his picket duty so that he could rest and that Martin would be happy to turn the handle to start his vehicle's engine. Allusions are made in the verse to the Station Officer, May, being of "countenance benign". Obviously Mrs Miriam Bayley was a tartar who guarded her cleaning materials with determination. Alan recommending the "languid ease and abounding beauty" to be appreciated at the Station, implies duty is rarely required. How different the truth must have been.

LINES TO A YOUNG MAN

Oh, won't you come to Station 39?
The atmosphere is really rather fine.
For it's run upon the theory
That the male sex is superi-
or to t'other, and that makes things just divine!

Oh, why don't you come to Station 39?
For the S. O. is of countenance benign.
And it's when the colonel's daughter
Brings you up your shaving water
That you feel as though the sun's begun to shine!

Oh, but please, please, come to Station 39.
It is better far than going down a mine!
Don't be bothered about picket.
Chris, Loraine or Lane will stick it
All night long, that you may on your bed recline.

Yes, you ought to work at Station 39.
When it's scrubbing day — that's Friday, wet or fine —
If the brush and soap evade you
Let our Mrs Bayly aid you.
"What, no brush?" she'll say. "O Lordy! borrow mine!"

Yes, you needs must come to Station 39.
For the girls to help you every way design.
If your engine isn't startin'
Don't get ruffled: call out, "Martin!"
Fingers fair will round the starting-handle twine.

Well, I hope I've sold you, "Station 39".
It's the station which supremely can combine
Languid ease, abounding beauty
And — occasionally — duty.
And if that won't satisfy you — you're a pig.

The third section of May's programme follows: a reflective record written in the style of an end-of-term report.

EXTRA INTERESTS

Several auxiliaries attend vocational classes and go to typewriting and shorthand, one to leatherwork and glovemaking and another to dressmaking. They do this usually as their short leave, though a little more time is generally necessary. Voluntary social work is also undertaken by various members among the personnel. One has been a most regular helper at the Beaver Club, doing canteen work on Monday and Thursday. The American Red Cross canteen is helped by another girl, while two auxiliaries go to assist in wartime day nurseries occasionally. Bed-making at the United Services Club is undertaken by one or two auxiliaries occasionally, when it is convenient for them to take short leave in the morning.

During the season various members went to assist with harvesting, not so often as they wished as we were short staffed. The Station also has an allotment in Regent's Park from which we are still enjoying cabbage and root crops.

For a long time the Station knitted furiously for the crew of a minesweeper, the H.M.S. *Corfield.* Unfortunately, it was sunk but all hands were saved, though dispersed. That, coupled with the difficulty about coupons for wool, stopped much of the work, but it still goes on in a smaller way and we send parcels of comforts whenever we hear from old members of the *Corfield.*

At the moment the Station school ambulance is at the repair shop, but for six months we have been responsible for the collection of physically defective school children for transport to Elgin Avenue School. This meant nearly two hours driving on the bus twice a day and also the cleaning of the vehicle twice a day. It is difficult to say anything definite about such interruptions as attendance at the A.R.P. School at Highbury, but periodically there are instructions to send two auxiliaries and an ambulance to collect from other stations on the way to the school.

The number of personnel on duty nowadays rarely exceeds ten in the daytime, including officers, so it can be understood that with cleaning and patrol duty, plus orderly duties and the fitting in of two hours privilege leave, there is very little time before evening for sitting down.

* * *

This resumé of the "Extra Interests" shows the extent of the voluntary social work undertaken both during the shift and on the following rest day. At least a few hours' sleep would be required after a twenty-four hour shift. One activity was carried on while sitting outside in the Mews, namely crews of both sexes knitting garments for the *Corfield,* as several of the photos illustrate.

Each year the Station entered an exhibition of art and craft made by personnel in their spare time. In one photo May is shown displaying her three stripes with the star above which denotes her rank. With her long plaits wound round to cover her ears in the fashion of the previous decades, she stands beside a model of a plane named "Sandy".

May recalls that Toms the taxi driver, who was a part-timer, had made an excellent model for the previous year's exhibition. "When I asked him what he was entering in the current exhibition, he replied:

'All I have made this year is a baby.'

"That does not count." I replied. "You have not used your hands."

'Indeed I have!' he riposted.'"

The crews were not allowed to leave the Station during the twenty-four hour span of duty without permission. However a short leave was granted of about two hours' duration during the shift if there were no emergencies nor likely to be. This short leave could be used to undertake voluntary work or further educational studies, as well as more mundane tasks such as shopping. The individual put in a request for a specified time which was granted or adjusted by Station Officer Greenup or Deputy Station Officer Dawbarn depending whether it was Shift "A" or Shift "B'. L.C.C. Inspectors might visit from County Hall to take a random call at any time during the day or night to check registers.

On April 16th, 1943, the Director of the L.A.S, Andrew Topping, sent out a memorandum from County Hall to clarify the number of staff who might be off station at the same time. Obviously this would cover staff undertaking regular duties such as visiting headquarters, collecting stores, attending lectures. (May lists many of the possibilities in the programme above.) This letter addressed to the Auxiliary Station Officers is almost apologetic in tone, merely requesting that the census of persons on site be registered on the following Monday, and forwarded to the area Superintendent.

This letter was sent at a time when the threat of air raids had lessened and the doodlebugs and rockets had not yet arrived. Station 39's personnel had dropped from a peak of forty per shift during the Blitz to a mere "twenty in day time". At night-time, part-timers would augment the figures. No totals remain for number of auxiliaries serving in the war although an estimate would be at least ten thousand. During the Blitz, Station 39 had eighty personnel divided into two shifts whereas Deptford, for example, had two hundred and forty auxiliaries.

The auxiliaries were allowed to take unpaid holiday leave of a week's duration each year. After May died, several of her holiday diaries were found, including one recording a visit to her father-in-law's home in Teesdale from the 19th to 28th August 1941. Looking through hundreds of May's watercolours the writer found eleven small paintings that matched the date and the text. The extracts which follow explain her fascination with the effects of light on landscape. Also, the trained auxiliary shows through when she writes that it would be unsafe to cross the river at a dangerous point. Her human side is detected when she becomes irritated by ten tourists and would like to push them into the river.

EXTRACTS FROM
MAY'S DIARY OF A HOLIDAY IN
TEESDALE TO VISIT HER
FATHER-IN-LAW IN AUGUST 1941

This diary, written in a college exercise book, was found after May's death.

19th August 1941.

Tuesday afternoon at last, and at 3.00p.m. the train, packed to the doors, drew out of Kings Cross leaving home and work well behind. Past the bombed town, through the lesser bombed suburbs, and northwards to golf links and then open country it picked its way until at last it seemed to shake itself clear of London and make for the north much freer and faster. Three W.A.A.F. corporals joined me for tea and their friendly chatter continued while the last of town slid behind us. They had been before a board for selecting officers and their comments, in abbreviated titles and initials, were very reminiscent of schooldays when one's world was smaller and self-contained. All had been in the Air

Force since "War September" and would not change to any other branch, but they all thought this length of service precluded the possibility of promotion, as they should have been singled out earlier if they had been any good. After tea they all went fast asleep and I was left to read my book, Vera Brittain's *Testament of Friendship*, undisturbed for miles. Undisturbed, that is, except for glimpses of the countryside which were almost nostalgically disturbing in one who has been starved of country living for so long. The grass was so green, the harvest so rich and, above all, the wide sky enormous and magnificent. This plenitude of cloud effect augured storms which broke at intervals around Peterborough and Doncaster. The effects of thunderous purple cloud, brilliant sun, very pale gold foreground, with purplish hills in the distance cannot be described; they can only be remembered and stored away in one's love of English countryside, in a store which has always been full of such effects — with wide skies always, and in the distance always purple hills, promising exciting views and asking to be explored.

At Grantham the "Air Force" left me and then the long flat journey across South Yorkshire began, with many crossings of deep banked slow-moving rivers — or is it only the River Ouse? Then came York and a great influx of khaki — and on to Darlington with a superb sunset to entrance one. The last ragged clouds were still illuminating against a pale green horizon, so typical of northern summers, when the local train left for Eaglecliffe at 9.30. Here my father-in-law met me and so we were soon at Normanby House. As we went up to the house, searchlights pierced the sky at every point of the compass and the air was full of a tremendous droning — British bombers leaving for Germany.

At four o'clock next morning the air was full of noise once more as the bombers returned. It brought the air offensive home to me as nothing yet has done. I hoped all the bombers had returned safely.

20th August.

Another wet morning dawned today, but soon the clouds went and the sun was brilliant. Yarm High Street was full of soldiers in full gas kit, including respirators, so once again the war seemed more real here than in bombed London. All afternoon the rain rained and the thunder roared round so I slept for two hours and felt most unlike myself for being so lazy.

Visiting the Dobson family occupied the whole of the evening. Patty was out and Tom was in the orchard, his back to a wonderful view of the Tees, busy cutting wood on a circular saw, home-made and driven by a conglomerate motor. A Morris radiator, a red Indian motor-cycle tank, and a battery standing alongside completed a weird but useful arrangement. The noise was deafening but he shut it off and showed me the produce of his garden. He told how he had just missed the bombs at Morton-on-Tees the previous night.

Mrs. Dobson startled me by saying she would not have known me until I spoke — but this is probably a change in her eyesight as much as my appearance. She was on a couch, an invalid but cheerful because the water had gone out of her legs again, embittered of things she had read in the newspapers today, when, she said, she should have been reading the Bible.

21st August.

After lunch we set off for Durham, by bus. It is an interesting ride through a country which is mostly rural, but with many reminders in the shape of small collieries. Durham's wonderful cathedral made a landmark, but alas, when we reached it the weather had changed and a steady rain stopped all idea of painting. So after a walk through the cathedral precincts we had a wartime tea, and then made our way to Elvert bridge hoping for shelter to sketch. Disappointed we left this fascinating view and walked to Pregeno's Bridge. There beneath the bushes dipping low, was the most perfect reflection I have ever seen; the river so still and the rain giving an unusual atmosphere and quality to the depth in the water.

22nd August.

With a wall sheltering me from the fresh wind I managed a sketch of Holwick, very bad and unsatisfactory — before walking back to the farm. The kitchen was filled with the scent of baking, pies, plain cakes, square fatty cakes and round currant cakes, all going into the huge oven in a constant procession. These were followed by mushrooms in milk after Sylvester and I had gathered them in the twilit fields.

23rd August.
A rainy morning dawned, bringing wonderful atmospheric effects. The road to Middleton is all downhill and very rural, with a wealth of flowers on the roadside and drifts of wild raspberries here and there. The town was full of visitors and after sketching by the bridge escaped again to the quiet of Common Top.

24th August.
Sylvester, a boy of fifteen, acted as a guide, a most interesting companion. The afternoon was given over to an expedition in Fairy Dell on the Yorkshire banks of the river. We explored a new reach of the Tees from Winch Bridge down over Scorberry Bridge, a narrow wooden affair with very thin stilts. It is a lovely stretch of river, pasture on the Yorkshire side and steep cliffs, woods around the Durham shore. When I see Sunday trippers I begin to wonder just how selfish I am, because they make me so discontented. A lot, eight or ten people, were scattered round the Little Force at Winch Bridge — I could cheerfully have swept them all into it.

25th August.

Another morning came blanketed in mist which at once thrilled and tantalised. It was a most heavenly colour but very wet — which meant painting under cover — limiting one's choice of viewpoint. Cauldron Stuart, like some mythical place had been my objective today but the rain rained so persistently and so hard at times that although we started we only reached High Force. A sketch of that was precariously achieved by means of sitting under a bush — very carefully unless one's movement shook down heavier drops than the rain made.

Sylvester did his best to get me across the river as I wanted to see Turner's viewpoint on the Yorkshire side; but the river was fairly full and every proposed crossing place had one stepping stone short! He said the best place to cross was as near as possible to High Force, but as a safety first person I would not attempt it. So we journeyed over a mile among the boulders with our faces meeting the soft wet air blowing down from Cross Fell. Once again the effects of the mist and rain were superb on the hills but with not an inch of shelter to record them. I really will have to buy an umbrella!

26th August.

Knowing there was a trip to be made to Middleton-in-Teesdale to meet the 11.30 train an early start was indicated, involving again a search for shelter as a driving rain storm drove in at intervals. So I sat in the cart shed and looked down the yard past the gate in the heights above Holwick.

It being Market Day the Taisdale train was crowded, although farmers have practically nothing to market. It is a sort of open air club there. As it was again raining heavily we went back to Common Top immediately and after a lunch of bacon and mushrooms and apple turnover, I went up into the hay loft to sketch from the open door looking towards Ash Hill Farm and High Force. During a fine interval we set out for Gibson's cave, a leisurely walk with time to love every bit of the view all the way. Here at the top of the cascade I did the third sketch of the day. In the evening I did the Italian view of two barns and completed the day with the stormy sky and storm-tossed trees round Common Top Farm. Would that every day could produce five such sketches!

27th August.
With extreme reluctance I packed my few possessions and said my sad farewells among invitations and promises to come again. Soon I was at Middleton-in-Teesdale and then into the train for Barnard Castle, after collecting my father-in-law from the gamekeeper's cottage. The usual rain beat against the carriage windows and stopped all views until we reached Barnard

Castle. Here again it was Market Day and the whole of the wide street seemed to be turned into a parking place for farmers' cars. There must be no poverty around there — everyone was well dressed. However my main objective was a sketch of the bridge and this was accomplished in spite of slow walking, showers and a spate of military. There were ragged clouds in the west, and the last remnants of a sunset which fitted better with the wild fells and cascades I had left than with the flat fields of turnips, potatoes and stacked corn around Nelly's Beck.

28th August.
My last day and I was determined to do least one sketch whatever other family duties I fulfilled. So after rushing down to the early post I set off along the the river bank and did a sketch of the turnips, potatoes and corn! with just a few willow trees and a stormy sky. The rain storm threatened by the sky inevitably arrived but the sketch was completed.

Before May became Station Officer she painted many views from the common room windows and her sketch books contain colourful illustrations of the buildings which are easily recognised to-day. "Clearing away Snow" depicts auxiliaries sweeping behind an ambulance while red flags flutter nostalgically. Unfortunately these watercolours lose their ephemeral quality in reproduction. Several of her paintings were exhibited at the Royal

Institute of Painters in Water Colours at 195 Piccadilly, and one receipt exists dated May 30th, 1940, for the sum of 21/-in respect of pictures numbers 82 and 483.

Reading through the programme of duties and knowing May's determined character, it is hardly surprising that for the last two years of the war Station 39 was the winner of the Efficiency Silver Cup in competition with the other Auxiliary stations — an achievement which bears testament to May's capabilities as an administrator. A photograph shows May and Enid Dawbarn posing in the Mews on their return from the award ceremonies on April 7th, 1943 — the year they were runners up.

The L.C.C. Minutes record that on October 14th, 1943, a representative contingent of the Regular and Auxiliary Ambulance Service was reviewed in Hyde Park by the Minister of Health, the Right Honourable Ernest Bevan. The Minister addressed over one thousand personnel and later took the salute as the vehicles paraded past. The Chairman of the Council was present. Several photographs depicting lines of ambulances drawn up in the Mews are thought to show preparations for this parade although no pictures taken in Hyde Park itself appear to have survived.

A sketch, illustrating a wartime slogan aimed at saving fuel and energy, depicts a bicycle being driven by S.O. May Greenup with D.S.O Enid Dawbarn holding her waist and Shift "B" Leader Marguerite Taylor balanced above their heads. A further four women cling to the frame while two more are towed behind seated in a child's truck as a third wearing roller skates is pulled at the rear. May sent this to Babette Lorraine on January 29th, 1993, a few months after she went blind. Writing in a cramped style, before she had the use of a writing frame, she enquires if Babette had seen this drawing before, and May ends "have a smile and remember the happy times, love Frances May alias Greenie."

The Dover Castle *(Kelly's Directory* gives the publican as Alfred Moyes) was the venue for the Station darts matches while table tennis matches were played in the Station Common Room. The Station also took part in a Brains Trust as a letter dated April 20th, 1944, verifies. Headed London Civil Defence Region at Group 3 Headquarters, London E.8, Mr C. R. Cartwright thanks May for her "excellent contribution at our Brains Trust, which proved to be quite a success". He continues that "your excellent effort in no small measure contributed to the success of the whole proceedings".

May treasured and carefully saved amongst her memorabilia many letters but sadly she did not remember the identities of the various authors of some of the more amusing, illustrated in verse. The first — the only one from this writer and undated — describes the white ambulance and illustrates it racing through red lights and flattening a cat. The third, fourth and fifth dating from 1943-44 are written by the same person. The drawings on the last one depict two smart ladies arriving at the railway station, their handbags spilling open. One of them is pictured on a crowded beach still wearing her tin-hat. The flying bombs or "doodlebugs" were responsible for damaging Jossie's studio. May was trapped in the wreckage: her back problem may have been a reference to this raid.

The second letter written on larger paper and the sole example from this hand, has been sent from Station 39 whereas the others are sent to the Station from either holiday or while away ill. Colour has been used to show May's face green from drinking plum wine. She rests at home with her feet on a stool, on the wall behind are several framed oils of nudes painted by Jossie. Elizabeth Bridge was his preferred model. Another delightful drawing shows three Americans shown waving and calling from their billet overlooking the Mews to the auxiliaries working below.

The Americans, drawn into the war in December 1941, were notable for their smart "officer-style" uniforms and the exuberant manner in which they approached all the female sex bearing gifts of nylons, gum and goodies from the P.X. stores. Many American forces were billeted in the immediate area: eight being killed by the rocket that landed near Selfridges in 1944. (Chapter 5: covers this raid.)

To welcome back the colleague from holiday, a washing line contains buckets, brooms, scrubbing brushes and a mat inscribed, "Welcome'. The fifth letter is written from the writer's sickbed. She mentions that there have been too many rockets going over for her to count and comments that if the Station has had so many they will have been kept busy.

In 1944, the Germans, having developed unmanned missiles, launched them on London by day and night.

The *Evening News* for Thursday, July 6th, carried the headline, "Flying Bombs kill 2,753, injure 8,000: very high toll in London" referring to the figures for the past fortnight. They reported that Mr Churchill, speaking to the nation a month after the first V1 flying-bomb was fired against London, said that between one hundred and one hundred and fifty had been launched each day. He said that the deaths represented about one person for each bomb. He ended his reassuring speech with the words: "London will never be conquered and will never fail".

The V1s were, in effect, flying bombs and looked like planes having a tail and fins. When the engine cut out the missile would glide down, allowing for a degree of warning. Over 9,000 were launched between June 1944 and March 1945 although only 2,300-odd reached the London Civil Defence Region. V2 rockets were different in that they fell silently from the skies. From September 1944 to March 1945, over a thousand V2s with one-ton warheads, were launched against southern England. However a former employee at the B.B.C. who was working for the S.O.E. in France by late 1944 thought the V1s the worse hazard:

"The V1s were, I thought, far more nerve-wracking. With the V2s you either were or were not on the receiving end. If they went off and you were alive, you were all right. But with the V1s you never knew where they would drop and the suspense from the time you heard their engines chugging over to the actual explosion was a real war of nerves. First I would try to guess how far off it was and whether it was coming over

121

my way. If it came right overhead without the engine you were generally safe. It was only when I went to Normandy in August 1944 that I realised, while sleeping for the first time in years without threat, what an unconscious strain it had all been."

May remembers that "we had to cope with the flying bombs and later the V2s which were worse as they gave no warning of their approach. One vivid memory I have is driving through a raid on Central London and seeing the flickering lights of the doodlebugs through my windscreen. It was a pitch dark night in June 1944 when we had been detailed to join a top secret convoy to an unnamed destination in the country. We arrived at Epsom Downs station by midnight to await a train load of casualties arriving later in the day following the Normandy landings on D-Day. Although it was June I was wearing my greatcoat and I remember that the night still felt bitterly cold. We had to wait without food or shelter on the platform until 4 a.m. when the W.V.S. brought round beef sandwiches and tea. My strict vegetarian colleague, Enid Simon, was so cold and hungry that she relented and stealthily ate a sandwich while imploring me: 'Don't tell on me, Mrs Greenup. I've just eaten a beef sandwich'."

Mark Arnold-Forster summing up fatalities for the war in *The World at War* describes the attributes of the flying bombs and rockets: the V1 and V2s:

"60,000 British civilians died in air raids of whom 9,000 or 15 per cent were killed in the comparatively short period during 1944/5 by flying bombs or missiles. These successful German weapons were totally indiscriminate, unlike bombers, whose crews would try their best to hit designated targets, the missiles, V1s and V2s as they were called, were simply aimed at London." A postcard dated 21st September, 1944, written by Alan Braley and sent to Shift "B" at Station 39 mentions the destruction of Wharncliffe Gardens by flying-bomb. As his earlier poem demonstrated, he was no poet, but the sentiments expressed are of interest. Alan on holiday in Worcester refers to his stomach pain and having enforced bed rest before he went on holiday. In fact, May said there was very little sick leave and few injuries, including her broken arm, for which she had only one day off following the injury. Braley alludes to the Station's "exploding mains" joking that Hitler might be interested to hear of their "bombshell".

Wharncliffe Gardens will not be found on a map today for in its place is Henderson Drive. The Gardens covered a large area of dwellings located between Cunningham Place and Lisson Grove running along St John's Wood Road. Lord's cricket ground lies to the east. Again the Civil Defence Indexes produced corroboration of the hit on the Gardens, recorded as Incident 705, from August 21st to 23rd, 1944. It damaged twenty buildings. Mr A. J. B. Fowler, an umpire at Lord's, living at 65 Wharncliffe Gardens, St John's Wood, N.W.8, relates what happened the day the V1 dropped:

"When the flying bomb fell on Wharncliffe Gardens, I was just inside the front door. This fell inwards on top of me followed by the gas meter falling onto the door. After picking myself up, I went into the living room to find a complete shambles of doors, window frames, glass and broken furniture scattered about. To my surprise, the only object remaining intact was a cricket trophy of mine which stands under a glass dome $10^{1}/_{2}$ inches high. It was not even scratched, but reposed in solitary state on the sideboard, the doors of which were hanging off their hinges. I have the trophy to this day."

Mr Fowler remarks that as umpire at Lord's throughout the war, he noted that play was stopped only once for one hour on August 24th, 1940, the field being evacuated by the teams, the Scouts and No. 903 Balloon Squadron. On July 29th, 1944, a flying bomb was heard overhead and the teams on the pitch from the Army and R.A.F. flung themselves to the ground. (May lived in St John's Wood at 118 Abbey Road, but the date of the incident in which she was trapped in the studio is not known. Wharncliffe Gardens had also suffered badly in September 1940.)

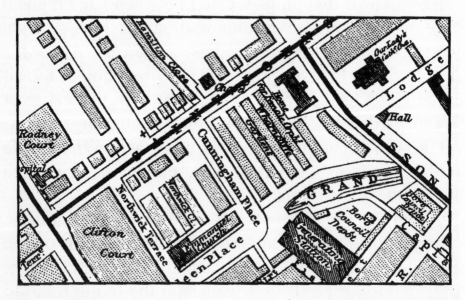

Wiped from the face of the map: Wharncliffe Gardens.

Mrs Wilkinson (who related Mrs Byrne's account of the bombing at Broadcasting House) visited her friend in Scott Ellis Gardens on August 21st:

"It was Mrs Byrne's practice to join some friends of hers, along with her two children, one-year-old Michael, and Josephine, seventeen years old, in Wharncliffe Gardens, a block of flats in the next turning. On this particular evening, I had called to see her and had held her up, making tea. Afterwards she was washing up the dishes, quite early on in the evening, when she heard a most terrific crash. It was the flying bomb which caused so many casualties. It killed the very people with whom, but for being delayed, Mrs Byrne and her two children would have been with."

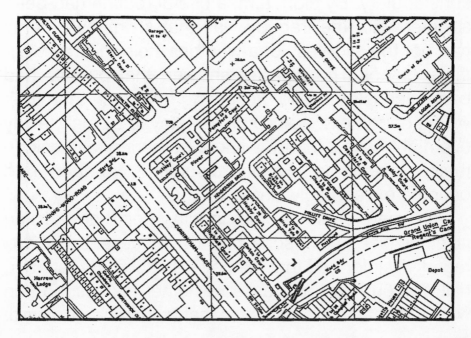

125

In the case of the Cinderella Dancing Club, there was no possible check on the identities of the young persons present except for members of the band, the waitresses and other staff employees. Within a matter of minutes of the explosion the W.V.S. set up an Incident Inquiry Point. Ideally enough, they found a room with a telephone only a hundred yards away from the dance club and set to work at once on the job of sorting out the identities of the victims and informing their relatives as to their escape, death or injury.

The room with the telephone was in the public library. Six members of the W.V.S. were on duty. The raid was still on. The scene was chaotic. But they took names and addresses from hundreds of agitated inquirers. They kept in touch with the police; they checked their information with the wardens and the constabulary. By eight a.m. a useful routine had been adopted. But the tragedy was that so many parents had not the slightest idea whether their children were there or not. The disaster showed that parents had been accustomed to accepting the fact that their young daughters — and sons — stayed casually away overnight "with a friend" without bothering to check on their movements. Family discipline, in fact, had become exceedingly slack.

One man came to the Inquiry Point and asked whether one of his sons had been present. He was regretfully informed that the boy was dead. He returned half an hour later and asked whether his second son was present. The answer was that he had been injured.

He returned the third time. By now it had been established that his third son had been killed. "My God! That's two of them," he said in a dazed voice. Incidentally, his only surviving son was crippled for life. An A.T.S. girl did not blink an eyelid when she was informed that her brother was missing, but when after three days it was established that he had been blown to pieces (he was a member of the band) she threw her arms round the neck of the senior W.V.S. and cried and cried. All that was to be found of the band were two or three pairs of shoes, and for days afterwards the W.V.S. had to sort out sacks of fragments of trousers and dresses for identification.

WOMEN IN GREEN, CHARLES GRAVES

Babette remembers one night when she was detailed to collect a plastic surgeon by car from the Harley Street Clinic. She drove him to South London where there was a scene of horrific carnage. A bomb had scored a direct hit on a hall where dozens of youngsters were enjoying a dance, causing many casualties. The plastic surgeon personally gave first aid to burns victims. She continues: "When we arrived at our destination, there were many people there, police, fire, ambulance, rescue teams, etc. I had to park on the side of the road to await the surgeon's return. Meanwhile many distressing sights were played out in front of me as teams collected what pieces they could of the youths' remains into body-bags." (No wonder some of the auxiliaries were plagued with nightmares.)

May remembered that on another occasion she drove to Paddington Station to collect wounded returning from North Africa. They had been detailed to collect a certain number of men and had taken several ambulances.

"Enid Dawbarn, my deputy, leaned over to speak to a soldier who had lost a leg: an identity label was attached to his remaining big toe. Perfectly made up as always — Enid was dressed immaculately in her tailored suit, smart heeled shoes and silk stockings, the seams straight — she smiled as she enquired about him. He responded with a laugh. However I was distressed to discover that another soldier had neither arms nor legs and was blind. Not knowing what to do, I asked him if he would like a cup of tea, to which he cheerfully replied: 'Could a duck swim?'."

CHAPTER
FIVE

Incident 707

The Civil Defence indexes for St Marylebone, lodged in the Westminster Archives, list and number all the incidents when bombs were dropped during the war. A folder headed "Weymouth Mews Number 39 Incident 707" contains hundreds of original "flimsies" which document the V2 rocket that landed on the Red Lion near Selfridges on December 6th, 1944.

From the first message announcing a "big incident", the action unfolds minute by minute. Having experienced five years of such emergencies, the lines of command ran effortlessly between all the services: Groups 1 and 2, the two Civil Defence areas concerned; St Marylebone Ambulance, the base for the local Control Centre; the police at St Marylebone Police Station, Marylebone Lane plus police dogs; A.R.P. Warden's Post C5 in Orchard Street; the National Fire Service based at Manchester Square; Depot 1 and 2 responsible for Heavy and Light Rescue services; the W.V.S. for mobile canteens, etc, etc. L.C.C. Auxiliary Ambulance Station 39 was responsible for deploying the ambulances sent as reinforcements.

DECEMBER 6th, 1944

23.20 From C5 POST in ORCHARD STREET to CONTROL: Priority. Duke Street junc. Barrett Street. Long-Range Rocket. Big Incident. Casualties. Report from roof of Orchard Court.

23.20 From FIRE BRIGADE at MANCHESTER SQUARE. to CONTROL: Priority. In vicinity of Granville Place, bomb dropped.

23.20. From MARYLEBONE POLICE to CONTROL: Services to Duke Street, the Red Lion by Selfridges.

23.21 From ST MARYLEBONE to GROUP I: Re telephone conversation. Police Station has asked for services to Duke Street by Selfridges. No knowledge at present of extent of damage.

23.22 From C4 WARDEN'S POST to CONTROL: Glass damage in Oxford Street west of Selfridges.

23.26. From CONTROL to DEPOT 2 and AMBULANCE STATION 39: Send 1 Light Rescue Parties. 1 Ambulance to Red Lion, Duke Street, by Selfridges Police Post.

23.26 From POLICE to CONTROL: Please send ambulance to Marylebone Police Station.

23.30. From CONTROL to STATION 39: Send to Marylebone Police Station 2 Ambulances.

23.30 From ST MARYLEBONE to GROUP 2: Priority. Damage Duke Street. Junc. Barrett Street. Big incident. Long-Range Rocket details follow.

23.31 From ST MARYLEBONE to GROUP 1: Down to reserves in Ambulances.

23.31 From DEPOT 2 to CONTROL: 1 Light rescue to Red Lion, Duke Street by Selfridges.

23.31. From C3 to CONTROL: Blast damage by L.R.R. Shop windows broken in George Street, Blandford Street, Manchester Street, Aynbrook Street.

23.32. From CONTROL to A. A. STATION 37 and DEPOT 2: Send 2 F.A.P., 2 Ambulances, 1 motor car. 1 Light and 1 Heavy Rescue, 1 Mobile Unit.

23.37. From ST MARYLEBONE AMBULANCE STATION (Lawn Road) to GROUP 1: Precautionary: 6 Ambulances to A.A. Station 39.

23.38. From AMBULANCE H/Q to STATION 39: Send ambulance to Duke Street, Barrett Street.

23.39 From CONTROL to WARDEN POST C5 and D4. Please contact Mr Sherringham who has gone to Incident at Duke Street junc. Barrett Street and inform him, Controller has appointed him as Incident Officer. He is to inform receipt of this message. Time 23.32.

23.39   From D3 to CONTROL: Blast damage in Post Office area. No casualties reported so far.

23.39.   From GROUP 1 to CONTROL: Re: your 23.28. Is there a fire?

23.44.   From FIRE SERVICE at MANCHESTER SQUARE H/Q to CONTROL: Please communicate with Gas Co.

23.45   From DEPOT 2 to ST MARYLEBONE: 1 Light rescue and 1 heavy rescue sent to Duke Street/Barrett Street.

23.45   From CONTROL to POST C5: Your 23.20. Duke/Barrett. Is there a fire?

23.48   From GROUP 1 to ST MARYLEBONE: Priority. The following services will be sent to you as precautionary reinforcements re Duke Street junc. Barrett Street. 2 ambulances from Station 19, Kensington, Station 26 and 28 both Paddington. To rendezvous at Station 39 Weymouth Mews.

23.48.   From STATION 39 to CONTROL: Return of 1 Ambulance from Marylebone Police Station. Police think should be sent to incident as may be needed there.

23.49.   From ST MARYLEBONE A.S. to GROUP 1: There is a fire, Duke Street. Feared many casualties, some dead.

23.53. From REST CENTRE CONTROL to CONTROL: Nearest Centre for homeless people is Weigh House, end of Duke Street. Tel: VIC 4765/ 3352.

23.55. From ST MARYLEBONE A.S. to GROUP 1: Priority. Please despatch immediately Loudspeaker car for incident in Duke Street.

24.00 From CONTROL to STATION 39: 2 Ambulances to Duke Street/Barrett Street.

24.00 From B.E to DEPOT 1: Send necessary poles and trestles to rope off Oxford Street/Duke Street/Barrett Street and Somerset Street.

DECEMBER 7th

00.01 From CONTROL (R.H.) to AMBULANCE STATION 39: Please expect shortly for Incident at Duke St. 2 Ambulances from each of the following Stations: No. 19 Kensington. No. 26 Paddington, No. 28. Paddington. Report arrival and do not despatch until instructed.

00.01 From ST MARYLEBONE to GROUP 1: My 23.28 Duke Street, Selfridges Annexe is occupied by American forces.

00.05 From F.A.P.2 to CONTROL: Could we have a car to take a sitting case to hospital?

00.10 From STATION 39 to CONTROL: Return of Ambulance from Marylebone Police Station.

00.13   From CONTROL to DEPOT 2: Please send immediately National Fire Service truck with lighting to incident Duke Street junc. Barrett Street.

00.13.   From CONTROL to STATION 39: Send 1 motor car to F.A.P 2.

00.14.   From CONTROL: Priority. Down to reserves in Heavy Rescue Parties.

00.17   From CONTROL to POST C5: for Heavy Rescue Officer. Your verbal request for National Fire Service unit with lights. N.F.S. inform me 21 lights with N.F.S. personnel are present at incident. Do you require floodlight units?

00.18   From STATION 39 to CONTROL: Repeat arrival of 4 Ambulances, 2 from Station 19 Kensington and 2 from Station 26, 2 from Station 28 both Paddington.

00.18.   From REPORT and CONTROL CENTRE to LORDS GARAGE: 1 Civil Defence van ordered to Barrett Street incident by M.O.H. personally.

00.30   From CONTROL to C5 INCIDENT OFFICER: I have 4 reinforcing Ambulances in hand to be made into 6. Please ask for them if you require them, otherwise let me know when they may be returned.

00.45   From MISS DARBY W.V.S. to CONTROL: Miss Darby at WEL 7514 and Mrs Bradburn at WEL 1479 for Mobile Canteen.

00.50   From CONTROL to POST C5: Please report present fire position urgent

00.51   From CONTROL to POST C5 for INCIDENT OFFICER: Do you require the dog? The sooner on the scene the better the results.

00.55   From CONTROL to POST C5 INCIDENT OFFICER: Understand that light mobile truck present at incident has no Doctor. If you require medical services for any trapped casualties inform immediately.

00.55   From C5 to CONTROL: A.R..P. Officer requests Mobile Canteen.

00.56   From. C5 to CONTROL: Re my 23.30 Duke Street. Electric repair party wanted urgently.

00.56   From C5 to CONTROL: Re my 23.30 Duke Street. Heavy Rescue Leader requests 6 debris tippers for mobile crane.

01.01   From ST MARYLEBONE CONTROL to GROUP 1: Priority. Down to reserves in Light Rescue Parties.

01.04. From BOROUGH ENGINEER to ELECTRICAL ENGINEER: Please send electrical repair party to Duke St incident urgently.

01.06 From CONTROL to POST C5: Please answer my 00.40 as to fire position, extremely urgent.

01.06 From ST MARYLEBONE CONTROL to GROUP 1: Initial appreciation of situation at Duke Street Incident, from the information available. Seat of damage is Island Site bounded by Duke Street, Barrett St, Bird Street, Oxford St, which contains small 4 storey buildings being shops with residences above and G.P.O. sorting offices.

Considerable blast damage in immediate neighbourhood which consists of Selfridges stores, West side and small tenement type property East and North.

Approximately 50 casualties; 10 of whom killed. It is thought American forces are probably heavily involved. U.S. Ambulances have been removing their own Casualties. Search is now concentrated radically from seat of Damage. All C.D. Services required have been so far met by local Stations. Situation is in hand, more detailed information will be sent as soon as received.

01.07 From C5 to CONTROL: Re Duke Street my H/R. leader requests one H/R party to reinforce 2 excavators already working.

01.07 From MARYLEBONE DEPOT to CONTROL: The lorry has now left depot for job Duke/Barrett.

01.07 From STATION 39 to CONTROL: Repeat return of 1 Ambulance from Duke/Barrett.

01.15. From C5 to CONTROL: Re your 00.40. fire situation nil. Only fire caused by gas main which is under control. Dog not needed.

01.15. From ST MARYLEBONE to GROUP 1 SURVEYOR: Please send 6 debris tippers for mobile crane to H/R Officer at incident Duke/Barrett.

01.16 From: C5 to CONTROL: Re. my 23.30 Duke St. Repair Party to sweep glass in Oxford Street. Needed before morning.

01.16 From POST C5 to DEPOT 1: Incident reported Duke Street junc. Wigmore St.

01.26 From STATION 37 to CONTROL: 2 Ambulances returned from Duke St.

01.33 From MARYLEBONE to GROUP 1: My 23.48 Duke St has confirmed that the fire was caused by a fractured gas main. This is under control.

01.41 From CONTROL to STATION 39: Please return 4 returning ambulances to Home Stations.

01.44   From CONTROL to GROUP 1: The following services will be required at Duke/Barrett: 4 H/R. Reminder: To relieve at 04.00 hrs. Marylebone Parties working at incident.

01.58   From C5 to CONTROL: Re my 23.50 Duke. 1 Light Mobile Unit returned to Depot.

02.04   From CONTROL to DEPOT 1: As you requested have arranged your Heavy Rescue Parties relieved at Duke at 04.00.

02.52   From CONTROL to C5 INCIDENT OFFICER: Can you now let me have a M1 together with appraisal of present position?

03.08   From C5 to CONTROL: Re 23.30 Duke Street. Gas repair party report all gas turned off in incident area.

03.15   From C5 to CONTROL: Duke/Barrett St. Casualties so far removed: serious 8. plus 2 American Army, minor 40 plus 25 American and dead 5 plus 2 American. (Number of dead does not include remains taken to Hill Road Mortuary.) Perimeter of structural damage approx. Wigmore Street North side, Oxford St South side, James St East side and Selfridges main blocks.

03.20   From DUTY CONTROLLER, ST MARYLEBONE to WEST CONTROLLER: Temple

Bar 0111 9689 3169. I shall be glad if you will convey to your officer concerned the grateful thanks of the St Marylebone C.D. Services for the spontaneous and valuable assistance rendered at the recent Long Range Rocket incident.

03.10 From I.O.W. SHERRINGHAM to CONTROL: Selfridges food store undamaged, other departments cleared for opening in morning. All casualties thought to be removed except those trapped under debris of Red Lion Public House. Confirmation will follow when gazetteer is checked. All M.F.S. have returned except 2 pumps standing by.

03.29 From C5 to CONTROL: Heavy Rescue Leader returned 3 L/R parties to Depot 2.

04.04. From C5 to CONTROL: Incident Officer wishes Water Board to report to him again at incident. 04.18. CONTROL ST MARYLEBONE to GROUP 1: Further to my 00.58 the following gives the present position of Long Range Rocket incident at Duke/Barrett St which occurred 23.08 on 6.12.44.

(a.) Casualties SERIOUS: 8 including 2 American Army Personnel. MINOR 40 (25 A.A.) and DEAD, 8 (including 4. A.A.)

(b.) Perimeter of structural damage approx. area bordered by Wigmore/Oxford/James/Selfridges main block.

(c.) Selfridges Food Store undamaged, other departments see above.

(d.) Roads closed: Duke Street, between Oxford and Wigmore. Somerset Street between Duke and Orchard. Barrett St. Between Duke and James. All glass removed from Oxford Street.

(e.) G.P.O. Sorting Office, Barrett St Severe structural damage. Armed Guard on duty. All Mail understood to be intact.

(f.). Incident Inquiry Point will operate at daybreak.

(g.). Generally 4 H.R. and 3 L.R. parties working. 2 Ambulances at stand by. 2 N.F.S. pumps in attendance at ignited gas main. All casualties thought to be removed except those which may be under debris of Red Lion Public House, Barrett/Duke. Check with gazetteer now in hand.

04.36 From CONTROL to C5: Mr King is appointed Incident Officer to relieve Mr. Sherringham a.s.p.

05.25. From CONTROL to GROUP 1: Duke corner of Picton Street. Gas Main has been cut off by Gas Co.

06.32. From the POSTMASTER to CONTROL: District Post Officer is asking if a mobile counter can be sent to No. 131 to 151 Great Titchfield Street, where the staff from G.P.O. Bird Street are now working as they have no means of getting food at such short notice.

07.08.   From STATION 39 to CONTROL: 1 Ambulance returned from Duke St.

07.31.   From L.C.C. at WAT 5000 ext. 6769 to CONTROL: L.C.C. inquiring re-damage to Barrett Street School. Mr Randall of Post C5 investigating extent of damage.

07.36.   From C5 to CONTROL: Re: 23.30. Incident Enquiry Bureau open at 07.30 at rear of Barrett Street School. Entrance Picton Place.

08.17.   From ST MARYLEBONE to GROUP 1: Incident Duke St. Extent of damage to Red Lion Public House demolished. Buildings imminent adjacent Duke/Barrett part demolished, also building opposite North side of Barrett St part demolished. Considerable blast damage to surrounding buildings including Selfridges, Post Office. Sorting Dept., Lyons Tea shop and American Army H/Q.

08.30.   From C5 to CONTROL: Barr Street School uninhabitable, considerable structural and blast damage on upper floors.

08.50   From C5 to CONTROL: 2 Trestles and large quantity of rope required.

09.05.   From C5 to CONTROL: Heavy Rescue Leader requires N.F.S. turntable ladder to inspect roofs of badly damaged buildings. Enter via Barrett St at James Street end.

09.29.   From CONTROL to C5: Latest casualty figures sent to me : 8 serious, 40 minor and 8 dead.

09.41   From CONTROL to C5: Revised figures: 32 serious, 30 minor and 13 dead.

10.10   From CONTROL to GROUP 1: St Thomas' School, Picton Place. Considerable blast damage to glass.

10.14   From. CONTROL to C5: Please let me have a.s.p. approx. no. of retail shops of all descriptions affected by L.R.R.

10.50   From C5 to CONTROL: There are approx. 150 retail shops affected by L.R.R.

11.23   From ST MARYLEBONE to GROUP 1: Revised figures, 13 dead, 32 serious and 30 minor.

11.36   From. C5 to CONTROL: Will Mortuary Van call at I.O. Point for parts of human remains.

11.45.   From C5 to CONTROL: Heavy Rescue require a lighting unit to be erected in order that work can be carried on through the night.

12.01.   From C5 to CONTROL: H.R. require an Acetylene cutting apparatus.

12.26.   From CONTROL to C5: Latest figures: killed 13, serious 32 and minor 30. Let me have American figures.

12.27   From CONTROL to C5: Will you please ask the American representative at Selfridges Annexe to ring Dr Bulman, M.O.H. at WEL 7766 and inform me when it is done.

12.29   From C5 to CONTROL: Casualties American forces killed 7, injured 26.

12.36.   From C5 to CONTROL: Light Rescue Leader requires 3 pairs digging gloves.

12.41.   From C5 to CONTROL: C.D. Van removed portions of bodies found at Duke St junc. of Somerset Street. All unidentified.

12.53.   From C5 to CONTROL: There is the likelihood that a Mr Stanley Abbott is buried in the debris of 39 Duke Street as he is reported missing.

13.19.   From CONTROL to C5: H/R are complaining that work is being impeded by American forces and workmen salvaging property from Selfridges annexe. Will you request Police to stop this work until rescue operations in the vicinity are completed.

14.41.   From C5 to CONTROL: 1 body, female, recovered from 39 Duke Street.

15.23.   From: C5 to C5 INCIDENT OFFICER: The following people have been accommodated at the Council's Hostel: Mr and Mrs Grey and 4 children from 27 Duke Street. Miss Hughes from 29 James Street. Mrs Miller and child from 5 Picton Place.

15.26.   From C5 to CONTROL: Civil Defence Van has removed 1 body belonging to Mrs Kiddell, owner of Red Lion. No other bodies out yet.

15.48.   From C5 to CONTROL: H/R require Water Board repair party. Cellar of Red Lion Public House flooding, impeding rescue.

16.14.   From C5 to CONTROL: Approx. 6 persons not yet accounted for in building.

16.35.   From C5 to MR. SCOBIE: Captain MacLean C.D.E. has offered use of R.A.F. Office Trailer for Incident Office. If you accept offer please telephone KEN 3431 ext. 92 a.s.p.

16.47.   From C5 to CONTROL: 1 further body removed from Red Lion by C.D. Van, female.

19.10.   From CONTROL to NATIONAL FIRE SERVICE. MANCHESTER SQUARE: Debris from

Duke St. being tipped at Park Crescent Mews Dump. Could you arrange Tilly lamp lighting. Confirm please. 22.53 From C5 to CONTROL: Body recovered 22.27. Housed temporarily at Barrett Street School C.D. Van required to remove.

DECEMBER 8th

05.43.   From C5 to CONTROL: H.R.S.O. Ducket of Station 27 relieved by H.R.S.O. Case of Station 28.

06.25.   From CONTROL to ST MARYLEBONE BOROUGH COUNCIL: State of Parties returned under normal Alert cont: Ambulances 6; Motor Cars 3; Light rescue 4 plus 3; Heavy Rescue 3 plus 3; Light Mobile Unit 1; Heavy Mobile Unit 1; Decontamination 2; Mobile Canteens 3 plus 1.

08.32.   From C5 to CONTROL: A kneecap has been recovered and has been placed in Barrett Street School. Should a C.D. Van be called to pick this up?

08.45.   From CONTROL to C5: Re your 08.15. Wrap up and retain for time being until C.D.Van is next calling.

09.00.   From C5 to CONTROL: As Warden-in-Charge of Tilly Lighting at Park Crescent Mews was recalled, B District should have been notified to provide Warden for Sherrylow Street dump. Your message should therefore be addressed to B District.

13.15. From CONTROL to C5: The following bodies have been identified at Mortuary: Ethel Florence Maxwell aged 28; William Percy Gibbs aged 41. Duke Street.

14.30. From C5 to CONTROL: Several articles from Duke St Incident have been handed in to this Post including 2 valuable fur coats. Will you please arrange to be collected.

14.45 From C5 to CONTROL: Is it possible to get some National Fire Service to help evacuate furniture from the Bunch of Grapes, Picton Place? They have a lorry standing by.

16.30. From C5 to CONTROL: There are some dangerous windows on 1st floor of Wigmore House corner of Duke and Wigmore Street. Liable to fall on footway.

17.00. From: H.E. NOBLE SITE REPRESEN-TATIVE to BOROUGH, ST MARYLEBONE: Rescue operations have continued throughout the day at Duke Street.

The site of the Red Lion Public House which was the point of impact has now been cleared and all casualties removed. The latest figures show that there are 8 persons unaccounted for but incidental parts of 7 persons are at present at council's mortuary. One further American has been reported dead. Killled 17; serious 32; missing 1. The incident has been closed down at 17.00. and will be opened at 08.00 hours tomorrow.

CHAPTER
SIX

Personalities

City socialite, cockney taxi-driver, concert pianist, telephonist, band-leader, cook, concert harpist, "tic-tac" man from the local dog track, Bond Street milliner: only in times of national emergency would such a disparate group thrown together for twenty-four hours a day gel so harmoniously. The photographs bear testament to the warmth of feeling amongst the personnel. However no photograph illustrates the trauma and stress felt by the crews as they pursued their gruesome tasks.

The following anecdotal thumbnail sketches of May's colleagues offer some background to these volunteers. She described how on sleepless nights she would lie awake recalling people's faces and the often humorous incidents of Station life to recount to the author by telephone the next day. Before meeting Babette Loraine, the only photos named were of Chris Finlay and Iris Harris taken by the Christmas tree. However, in early 1998, Babette studied dozens of May's photographs and was able to recall with confidence many names. Her own album included more named photos plus some delightful captions, and of the photos from both these sources a good cross-section from both collections have been

148

included. Often only surnames are recorded as first names were not used and others are remembered solely by their nick-names, usually a play on their surnames.

May wrote that "Enid Dawbarn, my Deputy was always smartly dressed in her tailor-made uniform and black silk stockings, as the photograph of her greeting injured troops returning from the North African campaign in 1943 demonstrates. Also the picture taken when we had been presented with the Efficiency Cup illustrates well the difference in our appearance: Dawbarn looks the part of the officer.

"My two shift leaders were Eileen Lamb and Margeurite Taylor. Eileen was a glamorous society girl with her own flat. Her father was in the regular Navy and her mother was on the Queen's working party at the Palace. Just before the war she had celebrated her twenty-first birthday party on the ship anchored in the Solent which her father commanded. He had presented her with a huge diamond ring to commemorate the special day but as she leaned on the rail pointing to a distant landmark, the ring fell overboard!

"On another occasion while going on leave, Eileen was travelling in a railway carriage alongside an airman who asked to use her lighter. As she lit his cigarette she accidently set fire to his magnificent handlebar moustache. She apologised profusely and he was gracious enough to reply that everything was "O.K." However she made the mistake of lending him her mirror. On seeing with horror the remains of one side of his moustache, he rounded on her: "That's all your

149

fault," to which Eileen replied, "Not, so. You're the one who should know about wind direction."

"One night Eileen received a telephone call at her flat which was near Portland Place. Having verified her name, the male caller informed her that he would be coming to strangle her. She, thinking it was one of her socialite friends teasing her, replied, "That'll be nice."

"The telephonist who had connected the call, having heard this exchange, interrupted to advise that Eileen report the call to the police immediately. The police, recognising the man's tactics, informed her that he had already been responsible for four murders in the West End. The man had invited women into air raid shelters for sex and then killed them. Eileen became understandably nervy about the threat: doubly so when the man, secretly stalking her, reported by telephone to her where she had been during that day. Eventually he was trapped by the police and subsequently hanged. L.A.C. Frederick Cummings was tried and executed for the murder of four women in 1942.]

"While this murderer was being hunted, two friends arrived to work at the Station. Everyone was required to share in mounting a continuous guard at night. As the garages were open ready for an emergency call, with vehicles standing full of petrol, a picket duty was necessary. The rota system operated with one person on duty for one hour. Pat, one of the two friends, admitted to me that she was frightened by the thought of the murderer 'going round killing people in the area' while she stood alone guarding the vehicles. I replied: 'You're going to be standing up while the murdered ladies were on their backs.' However I did offer Pat and her friend a joint two-hour picket duty which they gratefully accepted."

"Enid Simon," continues May in her diary, "a Jewish refugee from pre-war Vienna, was a harpist who played with many orchestras including productions at Covent Garden. She used to joke that during long periods in *The Messiah* when the harp was silent she would read a novel while the orchestra played on. She had soulful eyes and spoke with a quiet slow voice that went well with the sound of her harp. She cycled in from Hampstead and, on being reprimanded for being late for duty one day, she explained that she had been counting how many revolutions the wheels would turn without her pedalling. "She was a dedicated animal lover and vegetarian, which, she explained, had been due to the fact that her mother had enjoyed walking around Vienna Zoo before she was born. Simon (everyone was addressed by their surnames) adopted a stray dog that lived in the Mews, Jock the black Scottie. The cook came to complain to me one morning that meat had been cut from the leg of lamb cooked ready to be carved for the Station's dinner. She suspected that Simon was feeding meat to 'that stray dog'. When I questioned Simon she readily agreed that she had removed meat for the dog, justifying herself because, being a vegetarian, she did not consume her meat ration. I reminded her that crew members had donated her those extra eggs and cheese from their rations and in future no food must be taken until every member of staff had finished with the food. Next day, Simon, entering the common room carrying a lamb bone, proceeded round the room questioning everyone to ascertain that the bone was totally rejected. On receiving negative answers she awarded it to Jock. I had to laugh. Only once did she break her regime by eating a beef sandwich.

"On another occasion, Simon rushed in to report that she had dropped a screw into her engine while when she had been painting a small area inside the bonnet. She was frantic in case the screw was vital to the running of the engine. The screw had quite disappeared so I helpfully suggested that she turn the engine to see if it would start. As the engine roared into life, the wet paint sprayed all over the clean engine. [A terse note on her card found in the indexes states: "Accident to vehicle on 19. 6. 1943. Reference 174/43. To Blame".]

"One day Enid was despatched to collect a man from the workhouse and ferry him to hospital. She placed him carefully on one blanket and covered him with another. Blankets were at a premium and those in the ambulance had to be guarded assiduously. On transferring the man into the jurisdiction of a stern-faced hospital sister, Simon requested that her blankets be returned but the sister brushed her request aside. However Simon persevered whereupon the sister abruptly pulled the blankets out from under the sick man, hitting him in the groin as she did so. Simon was appalled and on returning to the Station insisted on making a formal written complaint against the sister. She had a wonderful spirit.

"Many years later, when I was living at Peewit Cottage near Moreton-in-Marsh, Enid Simon came to visit us when she was playing at Cheltenham in the new opera by Benjamin Britten. I asked her what she thought of this work, *The Rape of Lucretia*, to which she replied as she puffed her pipe: 'I would rather be Lucretia than play it'."

Babette, visiting Enid as she lay dying of cancer in a London hospice, saw a cat was curled up asleep on her lap. Surprisingly the staff had allowed her to keep it near her to the end.

LIST OF PERSONNEL STATION 39

This list of personnel who served at Station 39 has been compiled from a number of sources including word of mouth, captions in Babette Loraine's photograph album and from the incomplete index files found at the London Ambulance Headquarters. The date joined is the date the person started at Station 39: not always date of joining the Ambulance Service. Abbreviations: ASO = Ambulance Station Officer; DASO = Deputy Ambulance Station Officer; SL = Shift Leader; F.A.Inst. = First Aid Instructor; * Resigned; † Dismissed; ‡ Died; § Transferred to another station or service; ¶ Medical reasons or unfit.

Name	Joined	Status	Left
AIREY, Eily	28.12.39	Attend.	31.3.42§
ALDBURGHAM, Jocelyn Frere	5.9.39	Driver	4.3.42*
ANDREWS, Gladys Winifred	16.4.42	Attendant	

153

Name	Joined	Status	Left
ARDEN, Neal	3.9.41	Driver	12.11.42
ARDEN, Sidney	18.1.40	Driver	15.4.40§
ARMSTRONG, Doreen Mary	4.9.39	Driver	19.6.41*
ATTREE, Marjorie	11.4.40	Driver	12.3.41*
AUSTIN, Mabel Una	28.9.39	Driver	
BANBURY, Ella	13.12.41	Attendant	19.5.42¶
BARGATE, Cecil Vincent	1.12.40	Driver	
BARTLEY, Esther Margaret	1.9.39	Driver	29.5.42§
BARTLEY, Marietta Augusta	1.9.39		
BAYLEY, Miriam Elizabeth	3.9.39	Attendant	
BENNETT			
BRALEY, Alan			
BRUCE,	3.10.40		*
BUTLER, Josephine Florence Lily	1.11. 40	ASO	6. 6.42†
CRICHTON			
CROPLEY, Clyde Pembroke	15.9.39		
DARWIN, Sarah Monica	2.2.41	Driver	3.2.41*
DAUNT, Marjorie	31.12.42	Driver	
DAVIES, Joan Frances	18.7.40	Driver	6.7.44§

Name	Joined	Status	Left
DAWBARN, Enid Maud Proctor	1.9.39	DASO/dr.	
DJAKELLY, Tamara	28.3.40	Attendant	‡
DROSSI, Gladys Margaret	4.12.41	Driver	16.4.42§
EASTWOOD, Poena Moisenco	26.9.40	Driver	30.4.41§
ECCLES-HOLMES, Mary Hadley	2.9.39	Driver	24.1.41*
EDWARDS, William Albert	26.7.42	Driver	30.8.42§
ELLERSLEY EMANUEL, Simeon	24.3.43	Driver	
EVELIEGH, Albert Henry	8.2.40	Driver	18.9.40*
FARRELL, Blanche	12.3.42	Driver	6.4.42§
FARRINGTON, Kathleen	6.11.40	Driver	6.7.42§
FELBER, Rose Pat	22.8.40	Driver	22.9.40*
FENWICK, Irene Mary	8.9.39	Driver	13.5.42¶
FENWICK, Irma Mary	8.9.39		
FINLAY, Christina Margaret	29.8.40	Att/driver	
FISHER, Gweneth Bridget	3.8.39	DASO	3.10.40*

155

Name	Joined	Status	Left
FITZPATRICK, Anne Agnes	5.9.40	Attendant	22.10.42§
FLETCHER, Violet Anita	30.8.40	Driver	12.40*
FOALE, Mollie Lillian	2.9.39	Driver	4.1.40*
FOARD, Esther Clare	23.1.41	Driver	10.2.43
FORREST, Douglas William	18.6.41	Driver	19.2.42¶
FOX, Barbara Mary	1.9.39	Driver	10.10.41
FRIPP, Betty Agnes	17.10.40	Driver	6.7.42§
GABELL, Frida Margaret	2.9.29	Driver	4.41*
GALLER, Henry	14.8.40	Driver	21.4.42§
GASSON, Veronica Claire	17.7.40	Driver	27.3.42¶
GILBERT, Ethell Lenia	11.6.42	Driver	
GOUGH-THOMAS, Hugh	25.1.43	Driver	6.10.44¶
GREENE, May	12.9.40	Driver	31.10.41¶
GREENUP, FRANCES MAY	**22.2. 40**	**ASO/dr**	
GREENWOOD, Charles	18.7.41	Driver	9.7.42¶
GRIEW, Joseph	21.6.40	Driver	2.10.42§

Name	Joined	Status	Left
GRIMBLE, June			
Angela	10.7.40	Driver	29.11.40*
GUIVER, Beryl			
Gwendolen	4.2.44	Attendant	
HALL, Frederick			
Harold	23.05.40	Driver	4.10.40§
HALLIDAY,			
Louisa Mary	20.11.41	Attendant	16.4.42§
HALLPIKE,			
Lilian Lucy	3.10.40	Driver	
HARRIS, Edward	15.3.42	Driver	26.3.43§
HARRIS, Iris	28.12.39	Driver	30.5.41
HARRIS, Jane	18.12.41	Attendant	6.6.42¶
HART, Doris			
Lucy	1.9.39	Driver	19.9.40*
HART, Evelyn	2.10.40		
HARVEY,			
Arthur John	3.4.41		
HAZELDINE,			
Mary Gertrude	12.10.39	Driver	4.2.42*
HEADLEY,			
Kathleen Susan	19.8.40*		
HICKS, Christopher			
William	19.12.40	Driver	
HOOK, Betty			
Primrose	18.1.40	Driver	31.7.42
HOPKINS,			
Francis	30.10.40	Attendant	10.11.40§
HUMBER,			
Dorothy Mabel,	18.12.41	Attendant	4.3.42¶

Name	Joined	Status	Left
HURST, Elsie	5.9.40	Driver	22.9.40*
HYATT, Charles Henry	18.12.40	Driver	13.6.42§
KAVANAGH, Owen	17.10.40		
KEMPLER,	2.5.41		24.07.41§
KNAGGS, Betty Yolande Constance	13.6.40		
LAMB, Eileen		SL	
LANE			
LORAINE, Babette	22.2.40	Driver	
MAITT			
MARTIN,			
MONK			
ODDIE, Germaine Veronica	17.10.40	Driver	
OLNEY, Gladys	31.8.39	SL/Driv.	
O'NEILL, Mrs			
OTT, J.	27.9.40	Driver	*
PANNELL, Joan	4. 9. 39	Driver	21.4.43§
PARKER, Annie Ethell	8.3.40	F.A. Inst	29.1.42§
PAUL, Vera Agnes	28.9.39	Driver	31.10.40*
PEARSON, Joan	12.2.43	Attendant	
PETTIGREW, Katherine	15.2.40	Attendant	15.1.42§

Name	Joined	Status	Left
PETTIGREW, Kathleen Eveline	15.2.40	Driver	19.8.40*
PLANT, Beatrice	20.12.40	Attendant	3.3.44§
POLITZER, Ethell	2.11.39	Driver	4.10.40*
POWELL, Doris Elizabeth	27.8.44	Attendant	6.10.44
ROBSON, Monica Fairfax	1.9.39	Driver	5.12.40*
ROSE, Ursula Mary J.	1.9.39	Driver	24.1.41*
ROWLEY, Mary, Evelyn	28.9.39	Driver	15.1.42§
RUYGROK, Peter Maarten	15.10.43	Driver	14.10.44
SADLER, Wilfred William	30.10.40	Driver	28.7.42†
SCOTT, Anthony Joseph	14.3.40	Driver	16.9.42*
SEE, Edward George	4.10.39	Driver	18.6.40*
SHORT, William John Erskine	7.3.41	Driver	24.11.42§
SIMON, Enid Violet	25.1.40	Driver	
SLIFKIN, David Kenneth	21.9.42	Driver	15.3.43§
SMALLWOOD, Madge Ethel	14.5.42	Driver	
SMITH, Violet	31.7.44	Attendant	

Name	Joined	Status	Left
SPANNIER, Adrienne T.	31.8.39	Driver	
SPARLING, Joseph	17.10.40	Driver	10.3.42¶
SPARSHOTT, Ernest Harold	22.7.40	Driver	5.10.40§
SPEAKMAN, Alfred	16.11.39	Driver	30.12.41¶
SPENCER, Joyce B.	17.10.40	Driver	10.6.42
SPURR, Phyllis			
ST JOHN, Stella	30.11.40	Driver	
STEELE, Mary Elizabeth	4.9.41	Attendant	
STEHR, Hilda	24.10.40	Driver	
SWAN, Winifred	5.10.39	Driver	
TAYLOR, Marguerite	28.9.39	SL/driver	
THURSTON, Ursula	3.7.40	Driver	4.9.40*
TILLYARD, Alison Hope	15.9.39	Driver	5.42*
TOMS, Horace Charles	26.10.39	Driver	17.7.40*
USHER, Frederick Charles	28.12.39	Driver	11.6.42§
VERNON-WENTWORTH, Fred.	13.9.39	Driver	26.6.42§
VICTORSEN, Philip John	29.3.42	Attendant	24.8.42†

Name	Joined	Status	Left
VINE, Harry			
Matthew (Harvey)	7.9.39	Driver	25.2.42
VOWDEN, Alice			
Harriet Weight	23.9.39	Driver	30.4.43§
WALKER,			
Anne Margaret	20.5.40	Driver	26.9.40*
WALLER, Eva			
Grace Cameron	7.9.39	Driver	22.8.42¶
WELLS,			
Cecila Mary	15.4.40	Driver	20.11.40*
WILLSON,			
Winifred	17.5.43	Attendant	23.7.44§
WIRTH,			
Mary Emily	5.9.39	Attendant	2.10.40*
WOLFF, Roger			
Francis	1.9.39	Driver	17.6.42§
WOOD,			
Constance Sylvia	19.9.39	Driver	
WORBY,			
Henry Sidney	28.12.39	Driver	17.4.41*
WRAITH,			
Marianne Hurst	1.9.39	Driver	17.1.42§
YULE, Katherine			
Margaret Gordon	17.10.40	Driver	31.10.41‡

May continues: "Two other members of the personnel were musical performers: Joan Davies, a concert pianist and Phyllis Spurr an accompanist and piano forte teacher. When I joined the Station, Joan called out to me to ask if I was related to 'Greenup the painter'. Joan's husband,

Ivor Walsworth, a composer and violinist, worked as sound engineer for the B.B.C. premier concerts at venues like the Albert Hall. Joan regularly performed his 'modern' compositions. A tape exists in which she introduces her programme at the CEMA Hospital Concerts in a witty and interesting manner. Adrienne Spannier, a librarian, and Neal Arden, a presenter, were two more of a large number of B.B.C. personnel (Babette, too, after the war) who worked part-time at the Station.

"Our Station was fortunate in that no member of staff lost their lives on active duty: sadly though one girl did die. One of the six men who joined the Station when Mrs Butler was appointed Station Officer, became involved with "Peggy" [Katherine Yule], one of our younger, attractive girls. Mrs Butler and these men used to frequent night clubs during their duty periods and she had encouraged one of them to persuade Peggy to accompany their party. A colleague on lone picket duty, seeing them returning to the Station late one night with Peggy worse for drink, heard Mrs B suggest that the man, 'take the girl home and tuck her into bed'".

"Later, discovering herself to be pregnant, Peggy had a secret and, at that time, totally illegal back-street abortion. That evening her flat-mate arrived home to find her in a state of collapse and, although oblivious of the cause, arranged with her brother to admit her into the hospital where he was Registrar. As her father also worked at the hospital there could have been unfortunate repercussions when she died of peritonitis even though the doctors were not implicated in the abortion. Her death was a double tragedy since we never lost a crew member to the enemy. The man was promptly despatched on a week's leave to dampen down our concern for our dead colleague.

"No food was provided on Station while both the eight and twelve-hour shifts were operating. However when the twenty-four hour shift was introduced, canteen facilities were necessary. A cook, Mrs O'Neill who hailed from Northumberland, was engaged and rations were assigned enabling her to prepare meals. The daughter of a Baltic sea captain, she had accompanied him on many of his voyages: a fact that helped her to be strong and resourceful in the often difficult circumstances. Previously she had cooked daily hundreds of steak and kidney puddings for a well-known establishment in Bond Street. One girl was deputised as a catering auxiliary whose duties included shopping and helping the cook. The crews were provided with excellent meals through out the duration.

"One night, after a severe bombing raid, the gas and water supplies were cut off. Undeterred by this problem, Mrs O'Neill sent the girls out to collect fire-damaged wood from the local bomb sites. She made a fire in the cobbled yard of the Mews, erected a tripod over the flames and suspended a cooking pot from the top. As the men stoked the fire she proceeded to cook our dinner leaving the various pots to keep warm in the embers surrounding the fire. She said, 'Old Hitler would just like to think you hadn't had a hot dinner!'"

Iris Harris, was married in June 1941 to Stelio-Lucian Hourmouzios who was working at the Greek Legation. Babette remembers going to their wedding at the Greek

Orthodox Church and, afterwards at the reception, drinking thick, black Greek coffee. Chris Finlay, who prepared Christmas parcels for the children of the special school, was an Irish girl who was said to have, "the best legs south of the border" — not the Mexican Border but, in Chris' case, the border between Northern Ireland and Eire. Babette remembers that she smoked exclusively Balkan Sobranie cigarettes.

Joan Pannell and Babette Loraine, photographed together many times, were both good friends. Joan, nicknamed "Pan", resigned from the Service on April 21st, 1943 and joined the Wrens as a driver. Babette laughingly called to mind that if Joan had a puncture while driving some Naval officer, it was usually the officer who changed the wheel not the driver. She later married a submarine commander who was posted to the United States.

Babette remembers that Mr Maitt, a full-time volunteer who modelled the "Flit Coat," was most courteous towards them. He and his friend used to go to greyhound racing as well as to night clubs. He persistently implored the two girls to allow him and his friend to escort them to a night club. Repeated refusal became difficult so they agreed. Maitt advised, "Don't lose sight of me." They enjoyed the dancing and atmosphere amidst the austerity of their lifestyle. "The men behaved impeccably, being very decent in looking after us," Babette remembers.

May remembers: that "Hilda Stehr (Mrs Barnes), a part-timer, owned a millinery establishment in Bond Street, an exclusive location. Her pictures show her with stylish waved hair and fashionable clothes. Another girl, a buyer for Debenham and Freebodys, frequently had travelled to Paris for the company. Miss Crichton, another younger crew member, always dressed in men's fatigues with a white shirt and tie beneath, and her hair scraped back. The Station 39 group photograph endorses the fact that she appeared masculine. She also recalled that June Grimble was the daughter of Arthur Grimble, the author of *South Sea Stories*, a popular book of the period. When she was a child her father had been Governor on one of the South Sea islands."

Babette was reminded by photographs of several colleagues. Betty Primrose Hook ("Hooky") tried never to sit down, believing standing was good for deportment. Hooky, who left in July 1942 to get married to a Mr Suiter in Rhodesia, was given a leaving party. A photo taken in the Mews shows members of their shift sitting on deck chairs at tables arranged with food and decorated with jam jars filled with flowers. Another girl had a predilection for drinking neat perfume. One of the male full-timers always carried a prized solid gold case which held twenty cigarettes. When he went into the air raid shelter to rest he requested it be locked in the Station safe fearing it might be stolen if he fell asleep!

May continues: "From time to time I was asked to enrol special people; for examples a couple of 'conchies' [conscientious objectors] who were being harassed at another station and a young Dutchman extradited from the U.S.A. He didn't know London, couldn't drive and had no first aid skills so the reason for his assignment was obscure. Alan Braley, one of the conchies, wrote two poems about Station 39. I won't comment on their literary merit but as observations on the Station they are of interest. A rather mysterious middle-aged colonel was on the strength for a few months. The reason for his assignment was also obscure."

Babette remembers that Alan Braley and his friend repeatedly invited her and Joan Pannell to accompany them to Kingsway Hall to hear Dr Soper, a renowned orator. He was a Methodist minister who frequently spoke at Speaker's Corner. Accepting the invitation, they were installed in the gallery of the hall and entertained with champagne and the trimmings. They were introduced to Dr Soper which she found a memorable experience. She does not know why Alan was a conscientious objector but Jehovah's Witnesses and members of some Christian sects would regularly volunteer to work in potentially dangerous occupations provided they were not required to carry arms.

In 1942 Stephanie Currie, née Jones, the part-time auxiliary ambulance driver from Watford, was transferred from the factory where she had worked on Lancasters and joined the team developing penicillin under Alexander Fleming. The spore farm was situated in the British Moulded Hose Building, Sandown, Watford, until a V2 damaged it a few years later. She recalls being given samples of penicillin toothpaste and face powder to test. Everyone developed green areas where the powder had made contact. In retrospect, Stephanie says of the war that they had, "Looked to the humour to keep themselves going". She explained that she had thought herself lucky to be alive. She had no control over decisions affecting her life: she simply followed instructions.

May recalled that "at the beginning of the war, Kathleen, my younger sister, a trained nurse, was directed to work with child and maternity cases. However she had to give up her current nursing post due to contracting a severe bout of pleurisy. When she recovered she was assigned work in a daytime underground children's crèche. One evening she came home (she was staying with me at the time) with her clothes soaked with perspiration from the exertion of the job because she was still unfit. She resigned and having regained her strength later joined Auxiliary Ambulance Station 32 at Swiss Cottage in 1940. Of particular interest in the context of this account, her Station Officer was the wife of a senior official at the L.C.C. and a genuine Lady. They were close friends of the pseudo Lady Josephine Butler, my Station Officer.

"After a while Kathleen was sent back to the maternity care nursing in which she had specialised in the management of sick and difficult children. In her finals she had been awarded the best mark in the United Kingdom. Difficult primigravida were also dealt with in a no-nonsense manner by Kathleen. She told me of one instance when she was attending a headstrong society mother-to-be. During labour the woman insisted on going to the toilet against Kathleen's instructions with the result that as the baby was born it dropped down the pan. With great difficulty Kathleen managed single-handed to save the baby from drowning and cope with the now hysterical mother.

"In 1945 her agent recommended her as a nurse to Mrs Foster Dulles, wife of the American politician who was working in Europe. The Dulleses had recently escaped from Occupied France with their two sons, aged seven and two years old. The older boy Billy was in a state of nervous tension due to having witnessed the Germans' treatment of the Resistance fighters. The younger son 'Michou' was in a weak physical condition due to his mother's poor diet during a pregnancy behind enemy lines. At Kathleen's interview, Mrs Dulles announced that she was instructing her bank to place a considerable sum into Kathleen's account. Brushing aside Kathleen's protestations, she replied that she had been highly recommended and she trusted her implicitly. The money was to be used to purchase anything that the boys required for their well-being or comfort. Having established Kathleen and the boys in a hotel suite in Hove, Mrs Dulles then left with the instructions that the boys must never be out of Kathleen's sight as she feared a kidnap attempt. She returned, not within the promised fortnight, but four months later."

Kathleen worked at L.A.A.S. Swiss Cottage, where her station officer was a friend of the A.S.O Weymouth Mews who preceded May: Mrs Butler or "Lady Josephine'. The connection with her friend's husband probably ensured that initially Butler did not lose her job after being suspended "on medical grounds", since he held high office at County Hall. It was not until weeks later that a full enquiry was held. Mrs Butler never returned to Station 39 and subsequently, she was assigned a clerk's job at the Ministry of Economic Warfare.

May heard no more of Mrs Butler until a newspaper headline announced: "CREDULOUS SISTERS parted with £18,000 After Hearing Fantastic Tale". There followed one of the reports of the trial of Mrs Butler on three charges of obtaining money by false pretences.

While serving at Station 39, the report alleged that Mrs Butler alias "Lady Josephine" had defrauded four foreign spinster sisters of £18,000. She and her dog Kelpie had lived with them from 1938 until 1943. The trial was reported in newspapers from the *News of the World* to the *Evening News*. Mrs Butler was described as "a well dressed adventuress".

"In Court, the prosecution alleged that Mrs Butler had met the Misses Nina, Marie, Anna and Elsa Camenisch before the war, ingratiating herself into their confidence. When they evacuated to the country early in 1939 she was employed by them as a housekeeper. The sisters returned in 1940 and Mrs Butler stayed on as their guest until a few weeks before the trial. When she rolled up in her chauffeur driven Rolls-Royce which she claimed was "her Father, the Irish Earl's car," little did we realise this extravagance was funded by the gullible sisters. I expect she acquired from them the expensive and beautifully dressed doll that she claimed had been presented to her by Her Majesty the Queen."

Detective Sergeant Morris stated in Court that she had married her husband in 1932 but, having separated from him, her family had cut her off. At the time of her trial

169

she was living at Antrim Grove, Hampstead. She claimed to be the daughter of the Queen of the Belgians and an Irish peer, but it was reported that her father was a builder and she had been born in Iver, Buckinghamshire. However searching for the truth about Butler's past is to find it obscured by as many skins as an onion. She told the ladies that she preferred not to use her title because she was connected with the Ambulance Service. She entered the London Auxiliary Ambulance Service and was promoted to Auxiliary Station Officer but was requested to resign in 1942. No mention was made in Court of the reasons for her dismissal. She was also "the President of the London Amateur Boxing Club" and "Chairman of the Ambulance Benevolent Fund".

Mr Claude Hornby, prosecuting counsel, described how she had begged money to fund an underground movement called "The Pimpernel League" which was formed to sabotage the German war effort. She had explained that French and Belgian resistance fighters (as well as factory and transport workers engaged in sabotage) would benefit from these donations. Having extracted the first subscription of £800 from the sisters her greed knew no bounds. The League, she explained to them, was commanded by two Secret Service officers who, posing as Germans, would be transported to France. By fabricating that her husband, James, alias "Colonel Butler", was also a Secret Service officer she squeezed a further £5,000 from the sisters as a donation towards his exploits, namely going to France to sabotage the enemy's railway communications disguised, naturally, as a French peasant. Sadly James was described in Court as an unstable man with a heavy drinking problem which included even methylated spirits.

Building upon the fantastic story of the Pimpernel League, she pencilled herself into a central glamorous role. She whispered to the ladies that she was to be taken to France in a corvette with the officers. There she would destroy enemy airfields. Warming to her theme she introduced into her stories a Czech officer, Georgyevitch of the Yugoslav Legation. Naturally he had bone fide connections with King Peter of Yugoslavia — as likely as the allegation that she had been brought up by the "Churchill" family.

Fortunately the sisters" bank manager became suspicious and alerted Scotland Yard. One may question why it took him over three years to become aware that the ladies" accounts were being systematically drained. All the fantastic stories of the Pimpernel League were proved to be completely false. The money was never traced having presumably been spent on socialising and her extravagant lifestyle.

On being told of their house guest's perfidy, sadly one sister tried to commit suicide and the other three were assigned to mental hospitals. The prosecution had described the sisters as patriotic but gullible women. However Mrs Butler continued to weave her fantastic tales for the general public for another five decades. In the context of this operation, she had extracted at least £18,000 from the sisters: placed in the context of 1943, as Station Officer she had earned about £175 per annum but as clerk a little more.

Butler must have been devastated to hear her own counsel, Sidney Issacs, stating that "the time when lunatics were flogged has passed. This woman should be treated and supervised in a mental hospital, and then put on probation; that would be the reasonable and humane way of dealing with this case. Her life was unsatisfactory and full of repression, so she made up a world of fantasy as a compensation. This happened when she came to that 'remarkable house' with the unbalanced, credulous Camenisch sisters. She is not an ordinary criminal; she is not entirely responsible for her actions."

His plea did nothing to prevent her from spending a year in Holloway. Mrs Butler was convicted on three counts of obtaining money by false pretences, sentenced to twelve months' hard labour and fined £270 with £30 costs. Since this fine amounted to nearly two years' salary, the Court suspected that she had hidden funds.

May recalls that "during the period that Mrs Butler was serving out her sentence in Holloway, one of our girls, a conscientious objector, was sent to the prison for a fortnight to test her beliefs. Later, returning to Station 39, she related what had passed at Holloway. She had noticed Mrs Butler parading round in prison dress. Never at a loss for words, Mrs Butler hurried up to explain her presence in Holloway, namely that she was certainly no prisoner but gathering information incognito for a book she was writing. Pointing to her special red tie, different from other inmates, she explained this marked her special status to the staff; in fact she was but a 'trusty' prisoner working in the library. She could talk anyone into anything.

"A colleague, whose naval boyfriend had come home on leave, was treated to a dinner dance at the prestigious hotel Claridges, was surprised to see Butler, newly-released from Holloway, dancing with an RAF officer." Josephine Butler absorbed facts from other people's lives and wove them into fantastic stories. Probably copying the title "Lady" from her friend at the Swiss Cottage ambulance station and "Dr" for the convenience of receiving additional petrol rations are but two instances from a plethora of deceptions. By using her titles she was able to encourage subscriptions to her "good causes" such as the Pimpernel League and the Ambulance Benevolent Fund. By defrauding the Camenisch sisters of such an enormous sum of money, she was able to adopt the lifestyle that "befitted her position".

Possibly, on hearing May speak of the wartime exploits of her husband during the First World War, Butler embroidered these into her fictitious life. Jossie had been an officer seconded to the Flying Corps where he undertook sorties behind enemy lines to collect vital information. During the current war, May believed that her husband continued to collect information while visiting the homes of influential and wealthy foreigners to paint their portraits. The events following his untimely death in 1947 convinced her of his involvement in the Secret Service.

May Greenup had a formidable and charismatic personality which enabled her to integrate into the London life of the twenties and thirties. She was launched, following her marriage to Jossie Greenup, into artistic circles which included Dame Laura Knight, William Rushbury, Gerald Brocklehurst and Alfred Munnings. At the beginning of the war, Munnings, on being told by May that she had enrolled in the Ambulance Auxiliaries, invited her and Jossie to move to his country estate. Alfred hoped to prevent her "from wasting her artistic talents by picking up bits of dead bodies".

Personal relationships established early were maintained throughout her life as the hoard of written material bears testament. One example has come to light at the very moment of publication; namely a postcard to Kathleen from her employer, Mrs Foster Dulles, mentioning that she and her sons, Billy and "Michou" planned to meet May in London for lunch. Later May would be invited to stay in the Dulles' flat overlooking the Champs Elysèes. May enjoyed the luxury there yet she was equally happy camping. Touring in Teesdale during 1938 with Jossie, they were offered help in pitching their tent, May replied they only had sleeping bags. However, shelter was available in the form of their elegant Mulliner conversion Tickford drophead Austin 16.

She had a repertoire of jokes, often risqué, to draw upon, this reservoir must have stood her in good stead when she chivvied failing crews during low periods of the war. June Grimble said May's humour "helped ease the tensions, even though it was often of the groan-provoking variety". Up to her death she would always offer a selection of such jokes at the close of every telephone conversation, which was at odds with her nonagenarian status. Two examples were donated after she died by a friend who had treasured the letter for many years. Written in her bold hand but undated it reads:

An Englishman went to the Wexford Music Festival. He asked the hall porter for a newspaper and the porter replied, "Do you want yesterday's or today's?" to which the visitor replied, "Well, I should really like today's." "In that case," said the porter, "You will have to wait until tomorrow."

There is a second joke on the reverse of the page:
Two deaf men were travelling from Aylesbury to Baker Street on a slightly foggy morning. As one man looked out of the window and the other asked, "Is this Wembley?"

"No," said his friend. "It's Thursday."

"So am I," said the first man. "We'll have a drink when we get to Baker Street."

Doubtless she appeared daunting to the personnel at Station 39 yet they called her "Greenie" or "Frances May" when off station, and staff affirm that she was remembered with affection. May must take much credit that a group so varied in social and economic background worked together so efficiently. She tempered her determination with compassion.

CHAPTER
SEVEN

Victory Celebrations

Auxiliary Stations began to be shut down soon after the German rocket sites had been captured by the invasion forces, and May said that Station 39 was the last of the one hundred and thirty-nine Stations to close. According to the L.C.C. Minutes, approaching disbandment the full-time auxiliaries in service numbered 1,200 with 883 in the part-time contingent. An official group photograph of Station 39's personnel illustrates twenty-nine full timers at closure. Before any closures were implemented, a Ceremonial Parade with representatives from each station was held. Preparations of the vehicles had been extensive and super thorough. For the last time the ubiquitous ladder, seen propped against the wall in many of the photos, was utilised to enable the top of the ambulance's roof to be cleaned. The route taken was by "deadly" slow process around Regent's Park and through Hyde Park. Babette remembers that this was the last drive they had in a column. Returning to the Station, she engraved the letters R.I.P. on the facia of her trusty ambulance: a farewell to arms for DXP 943.

Superintendent John Rees wrote an appreciative personal letter to May about the time that the Station was closed down in which he thanked her for rescuing the Station "twice at a critical period". The first instance was in the early days of the Blitz when May was temporarily given command after the Misses Bruce and Fisher had fled. The second, far more serious, referred to the problems experienced with Josephine Butler. According to May, this problem was but the tip of an iceberg of theft and deceit that undermined not only Station 39 but the Ambulance Benevolent Fund and the London Amateur Boxing Club as well as threatening the careers of the Ambulance Service personnel and County Hall officials. Besides whatever monies accrued in Butler's private bank account from the cheques destined for the bodies mentioned and the Pimpernel League, one must not forget the four sisters who were defrauded. It is worth remembering that these monies — totalling some £18,000 were never traced: Lady Butler had frittered it away on high living and gifts. And May later discovered thousands of stubs from ticket sales in aid of the London Amateur Boxing hidden away in a cupboard.

May remarked that one official from County Hall told her that if the Butler bubble had not burst when it did he could not have escaped involvement. Having accepted gifts from Butler for favours arranged, he would have been part of the proceedings. May hinted that the officials at County Hall "as far as the top" were implicated in the enquiry but, although giving clues, she named no names. No doubt such disciplinary interviews that were held were not minuted or, if minuted, would have restricted access or maybe they were just "lost in the bombing".

On July 1st, 1945, the L.C.C. issued the following message:

"The Council expresses warm appreciation of the good work done during the war by the Regular and Auxiliary Ambulance Service.

The Ambulance Museum at Ilford exhibits a personal letter written by Queen Elizabeth on behalf of the King and herself, which expresses their appreciation for the wartime service.

May explains that towards the end of the war everyone was allowed a railway voucher for return travel to anywhere in the United Kingdom. As Elizabeth Bridge, who was serving in the Fire Service, also had privilege leave, they both went to the Lake District for three days. May mentioned that they completed several water colours each.

Looking back May remarked that "the war lasted a very long time — five and a half years — but I made many friends and learned a lot so I recall the time with some pleasure."

In a nostalgic letter to Babette Loraine on May 7th, 1983, she wrote:

"My Dear Loraine,
"It must have been all this furore about '40 years ago' which made me think I would like to speak with you — you being one who joined the Service the same day as me and lasted the whole of the five and a quarter years.

"Well, if I spoke to you I could only say that knowing you was one of the good things which came from the long years at Station 39. Sometimes reflecting on various episodes I cannot imagine how we survived! Perhaps one should try to remember only the cheerful and amusing things and there were certainly plenty of those from time to time. Whatever it was, it was certainly an unique part of my life and one I would not have chosen to miss even though a great deal was a sort of,

"They also serve who only stand and wait."

Frances."

The full story of the courage and devotion to duty of the ambulance staff during the aerial attack on London can never be told. The few instances which we record below are selected from a mass which have been reported to the headquarters of the ambulance service; they are merely a representative selection. But in addition to these there must have been many hundreds equally meritorious which have never come to light, either because eyewitnesses other than the chief participants were not present, or because all who took part regarded such deeds of courage as the commonplaces of warfare which did not call for comment or report.

An ambulance attendant was called one night to an "incident" in which a number of people were trapped in the basement of a house; she descended to the basement and pushed her way under a heap of debris where, under a doctor's orders, she was able to give a hypodermic injection to a man whose legs were pinned under slabs of concrete. On one side of the patient was a dead body and on the other side an injured woman was also trapped. The only support for the ambulance attendant were two drain pipes: she remained two hours supporting the patient until he could be released.

Two men auxiliaries were sent to collect casualties at premises where a big fire was raging; the road leading to the building was blocked by a sheet of flame. Without hesitation they drove the ambulance through the fire and, with the help of a policeman, loaded the stretchers with casualties; the heat was so intense that the stretchers were almost too hot to handle. After being warned to get away before the building collapsed, which in fact it did just after they left, they got the patients safely to hospital and reported back to their station for further duty.

During the early part of the Blitz, when Silvertown and district was subjected to intense bombardment, there was pressure on the local services. Ambulances were sent from London, and in this unfamiliar territory a woman driver and her attendant were driving in convoy behind three other ambulances when the first three refused to proceed owing to the fire and bombardment. The two women proceeded with their own vehicle and led a convoy into the danger area, where they were able to evacuate women and children rendered homeless by enemy action. They made five journeys to and from the affected area, taking the victims to safety.

In April, 1941, a land mine destroyed the school in which a South London ambulance station was housed; at the same time other bombs set fire to the adjoining buildings and partly blocked the entrance to the shelter. A woman ambulance attendant, who was responsible for receiving telephone messages for the despatch of ambulances, went to the telephone in the wrecked office; she had to lie under the table in order to reach the instrument, and in this position, after considerable delay, succeeded in making contact with the control room. When she was ultimately ordered to leave the premises and take up duty at another ambulance station she continued her work and helped in the collection of casualties in the neighbourhood.

During an air raid in April, 1941, a male auxiliary was detailed to go to a major incident where people were buried beneath debris. It appeared at first sight that the casualties could not be reached, but this auxiliary made an attempt to rescue some of the victims. He forced his way into the basement and enabled a woman doctor to follow him and administer morphia to women who were pinned under beams and debris. With the help of others who afterwards volunteered, they were able to release these people, and got them to hospital.

One of the earliest losses in the ambulance service occurred when two vehicles were standing-by at a scene of an incident in Holborn when further bombs fell and completely destroyed the personnel and their vehicles. No trace of the four victims was ever discovered except some small articles of personal property.

Many ambulance stations were hit by bombs, and not a few were totally destroyed. One station in the Isle of Dogs received a direct hit which reduced the building to ruins and killed eight of the staff. In the ambulance service, as elsewhere, there were many miraculous escapes. Two stations in Shoreditch were demolished by land mines. To those who saw the ruins in daylight on the following morning it seemed incredible that any of the occupants could have remained alive, but in fact none suffered more than relatively slight injuries. Immediately after the incident at one of the stations two of the women staff carried the casualties to hospital in one of the few vehicles which was still usable but which had neither sides nor roof.

A driver in the regular service was conveying a child and nurse along a south London road during an air raid when numerous bombs were falling in the neighbourhood. A high explosive bomb dropped close to the ambulance, which sustained extensive damage; the driver managed to bring it to a standstill, and, although suffering from facial injuries and severe shock, he rendered assistance to the unconscious nurse, who was pinned in a corner of the ambulance by a large piece of curbstone weighing three cwt. He then returned to the station in a passing laundry van and arranged for another ambulance to pick up the injured nurse and the child, who were then conveyed to hospital.

LONDON COUNTY COUNCIL REPORT, 1944

AWARDS TO MEMBERS OF THE LONDON AUXILIARY AMBULANCE SERVICE

George Medal

George Goshawk, Attendant, Station 126,
Bertram Matthewman, Driver, Station 126,
During an air raid, Mr. Matthewman and Mr. Goshawk left with an ambulance to pick up casualties at premises where a big fire was raging. The road leading to the building was blocked by a sheet of flame. Without hesitation they drove the ambulance through and, with the help of a policeman, loaded the stretchers with casualties. The heat was so great that the stretchers were almost too hot to handle. After being warned by the policeman to get away before the building collapsed, which in fact it did just after they left, they got their patients safely to hospital and reported back to their station for further duty. Both men displayed splendid courage and devotion to duty. [March 1941]

Edward Morrison, Driver, Station 149
Three women were trapped in the basement of a demolished house. Mr. Morrison volunteered to rescue them and scrambled through a hole in the wreckage where he found the women trapped under a beam. The only way Mr. Morrison could lift it was to crawl under one end and, taking the full weight of it on his shoulders, force it up sufficiently to release the victims. Debris was continually falling, but after nearly three hours' work the casualties were brought out safely. [September 1941]

British Empire Medal

Mabel Ann Armitage, Attendant, Station 54
Betty Leverton, Attendant, Station 54
Philip Davey, Attendant, Station T.S.5
Ruby Gwendoline Sandford, Attendant, Station T.S.5
Joseph Slipman, Attendant, Station T.S.5
George Frederick William Tindall, Attendant, Station T.S.5

Ambulances were sent to evacuate women and children rendered homeless by enemy action who were in grave danger. Owing to intense fires only three ambulances were able to get through. Driven and attended by the members of the staff referred to, these ambulances formed a convoy and made five journeys to and from the affected area taking the victims to safety. [May 1941]

Miss R. J. Campbell, Auxiliary Station Officer, Station 141
For untiring devotion to duty on civil defence work. [June 1941]

Miss V. M. Cowper-Smith, Auxiliary Station Officer, Station 148,
For untiring devotion to duty on civil defence work. [June 1941]

Hilda Lilian Watts, Auxiliary Station Officer, Station 180
Untiring devotion to duty on civil defence work. [June 1942]

Commendation

Helen Annie Mason, Attendant, Station 11
Brave conduct in civil defence. [March 1941]

Lucy Elisabeth Hedges, Driver, Station 40
On the night of 16th-17th April, 1941, when, although seriously injured in the head and legs as a result of enemy action, Mrs. Hedges did everything in her power, with complete disregard of her own injuries, to see that another ambulance was despatched to deal with casualties for whom she had been waiting when she was injured. [July 1941]

Lilian Upcott, Deputy Auxiliary Station Officer, Station 165
On the night of 16th-17th April, 1941, when, after her ambulance station had been seriously damaged by enemy action, Miss Upcott carried on the work of the station from a wrecked office where the only telephonic communication with Borough Control was available. Later Miss Upcott moved records, personnel and vehicles to another station and then went out and acted as an attendant on an ambulance. [July 1941]

Margaret Wood, Driver, Station 90
Dora Shadbolt, Driver, Station 90
On 17th April, 1941, when Auxiliary Ambulance Station No. 90, at Edmund Halley School, N.1, was demolished by enemy action, although suffering from shock, Miss Wood and Miss Shadbolt assisted some of their injured

colleagues to the shelter and then drove some of them to hospital in an ambulance, the sides and top of which had been blown off. After receiving treatment they drove the ambulance back to the station. [September 1941]

CHAPTER
EIGHT

Postscript

During the spring of 1983, May, reading quietly, was disturbed by the telephone. She heard Babette Loraine request her to switch on her radio immediately as Libby Purves was interviewing a Dr Josephine Butler — their very same disgraced station officer — about the launch of her book, *Churchill's Secret Agent*. A panel of eminent guests had been invited to discuss with her the veracity of her claims that during the war she was an intelligence agent responsible only to Prime Minister Winston Churchill. Relating how Churchill had recruited eleven other agents besides herself, she explained they remained unknown to each other. The individuals that made up this "Secret Circle" were despatched on top secret missions behind enemy lines. This fabrication was reminiscent of the Pimpernel League fantasy that Butler related to the Camenisch sisters in 1942 in order to extract their donations, "for her own use and for something she would not discuss".

Challenged about the authenticity of facts presented in her book by a suspicious media, May and Babette heard her state that neither MI5 nor the War Office knew of the existence of the Secret Circle. Her only contact, Butler explained, had been with a major working incognito who had escorted her to private briefings with the Prime Minister. Installed in a flat in Sloane Street, her whereabouts unknown even to her family, Butler claimed that she spent the last four years of the war involved in over fifty drops behind enemy lines. Her brief was to glean vital information which she relayed directly to Churchill by radio and on her return from France.

In the book, Butler paints an exaggerated portrait of herself as a superwoman, a female 007, whose exploits sweep the reader along. *Churchill's Secret Agent* does offer "a jolly good read" in the words of her publisher, being a derivative of the B.B.C. television series which related the adventures of English agents working with the Resistance in France. However the Gestapo officers who interrogated her rely for role models more on officers in the *'Allo, 'Allo* series. Her claim to be proficient in jujitsu and karate, an athlete, pilot, horse-woman and ace driver (she had forgotten she was unable to drive) is incompatible with the picture of the rather flat-footed forty-year-old photographed alongside her colleagues at the Ambulance Station in 1941, when the "Lady Josephine" story broke. Neither Butler's "sex appeal" nor "long shapely legs" (described in her book) are in evidence. However, according to her statement, this impressive list of athletic prowess stood her in good stead when a well-known circus clown was given the task of teaching her how to jump from a Lysander travelling at five feet above the ground.

Following the radio interview, an article by Tony Conyers appeared in the *Daily Telegraph* on April 20th, 1983 which ridiculed Butler's story of the Secret Circle and her exploits in France. He reported that Group Captain Hugh Verity (who had piloted twenty-nine Lysander missions) succinctly refuted the claim that a person could jump from a Lysander which was flying five feet above the ground — anyone foolish enough to attempt this stunt, he stated categorically, would be decapitated by the tailplane. Butler's claim that Klaus Barbie of the Gestapo interrogated her in Paris was also shown to be false since he was in Lyons at the time.

Conyers interviewed Butler and she declined to speak French even though she claims in her book that French was her first language since she was a pupil at a Belgian convent from the age of eight, (banished from home for "attacking a carter") and not returning to England until she was thirty-six. Always resourceful, she explained away her inability to speak French to her interviewers as a plain refusal because, "General de Gaulle had made insulting remarks about Winston Churchill and the English at a private function in London in 1969".

Butler was becoming a notorious charlatan to historians: later to be one of the subjects in *Counterfeit Spies* (St Ermin's Press, 1998) by Nigel West, an expert in the field. Analysing her fantastic claims, West states that the highest number of missions to France undertaken by a SOE agent was seven; the norm was two, making the total of seventeen missions that Butler discusses in her book unbelievable. On the dustjacket of her book she states that she flew on more than fifty missions. Discussing her claim that she was flown in Lysanders from Tempsford, West states that her missions are not logged "in the RAF's copious records".

Nor is there entry of any pilot killed returning from France on May 16th, 1944 as Butler alleges. Even her publisher, John Shillingford of Blaketon Hall, was quoted as having misgivings as to whether the book should be classified as fact or fiction.

Babette sent a cassette recording of the Purves' radio interview to May who had not heard it in full and asked her to request a copy of the book from her local library. When returning the tape, May commented on Butler's habit of talking everyone down in conversation:

May 27th, 1983.

"Dear Babette,

"At last the tape has been heard, and very interesting too. As ever the 'Lady' talked over everyone and managed very cleverly to avoid giving any real information.

"I must say that I would not have thought it was Josephine's voice as some of the words sounded quite affected. On the back of the book cover is a current photograph in which her neck is hidden by a large scarf so she may have had some throat trouble. Perhaps the second jaw she is growing affects her speech or perhaps, as our helper who lent me the tape player said, she was making herself sound 'a bit posh'. Whatever the voice, the drift and attitude to everything is the same. You asked me if her name was Josephine and on wartime records she was Florence Lily, also given in the account of the law court proceedings. Curiously in her book she says that that was her 'cousin double's' name. I have two or three old newspaper cuttings — the *News of the World* for one, in which you featured among them. They all mention that she said she was helping to train men for the Second Front to help Winston, but the judge said she lived in a fantasy world.

"Her book skims over the first three years of the war and begins in 1943 when she allegedly substituted her cousin in her job at the Ministry of Economic Warfare and apparently they played box and cox for the rest of the war! Apparently the publisher of the book said he did not know whether to publish it as fact or fiction. All the way through there is no one mentioned who could corroborate anything. Perhaps only finger prints could do that. It leaves one guessing.

"I have returned the tape under separate cover and thank you for letting me hear it. With this I am enclosing a few snaps of the Ambulance Station and if you already have any similar please dispose of these as they are duplicates.

"Like you I have many mixed memories of those five years but if I stay to record them you will get eye strain and I shall have writer's cramp and, furthermore, this letter would be greatly delayed. It will have to wait until we meet which may be this year. I will telephone the coach station to discover what the summer timetable is. That would be the simplest journey, but if it does not prove possible then Moreton-in-Marsh is only about seven miles away."

When Nigel West's book was published in 1998, he was unaware that Butler was at L.A.A.S. Station 39 from October 1940 until her ignominious dismissal, or that she then called herself Florence Lily, as she was named at her trial in 1944, as well as admitting to the title of

"Lady Josephine". At the time, West was cynical about the titles of Lady and Doctor but had no evidence to totally disprove them. As we have seen, both these forms of address were used by Butler to get petrol above the ration or as a front for the swindles to raise money. Until now, the connection between the post-war authoress Josephine Butler and the fraudulent wartime station officer Florence Lily Butler has not been made.

The critical evidence which proves beyond doubt that Butler's titles were spurious are the reports of her prosecution in February 1944. Nothing had connected Butler to criminal activities until the author found May Greenup's press cuttings. Had Nigel West known that Butler had been sentenced to hard labour at Holloway, not only for deception but for fraudulently stealing money from the Camenisch sisters, a completely different complexion could have been put on the claims in her book. In 1942 her cruel behaviour caused one of the sisters to attempt suicide and consigned three to a mental institution.

Butler's flight of fantasy imagining herself being made to clean out latrines for the Gestapo at the Avenue Kleber probably echoes her similar tasks while an inmate at Holloway. Certainly comparisons can be drawn between "her six men" who she brought to Station 39 and the imaginary group of "Resistance fighters" she claimed to have trained in France.

Butler relates in *Churchill's Secret Agent* that she has a cousin, Florence who takes her place at the Ministry of Economic Warfare when she is in France working undercover. May refers in her letter to the curious fact that Butler gives her "cousin" her own name. Butler invents this cousin (nicknamed "Jo", being Butler's double) who has married Butler's husband's brother: both ladies conveniently share the same surname. That the cousins were identical is explained by the story that Butler was the daughter of an Irish earl and the Queen of the Belgians, who had a twin sister — Jo's mother. (Butler seems not to have realised such a liaison would have rendered her illegitimate with no "title"). These aristocratic connections were reinforced to the personnel at Station 39: "a doll had been presented by the Queen" and "I have close connections at the very highest level". Butler refused throughout her life to divulge her maiden name. Even when, as Nigel West states, her prospective publishers, David and Charles, had announced a sensational pre-publication scoop in March 1982 as "the wartime story of the respected physician and cancer specialist", she was adamant in refusing to give her maiden name causing the publishers to abandon the deal. On her death certificate a line is carefully drawn in the space for maiden name but her date of birth is given as December 25th, 1901. Acting upon the assumption that the date given in her book and repeated on the certificate was correct, application was made to Iver and Langley in Buckinghamshire recorded as her place of birth but the Registrar searched a wide area without success.

A trawl was then undertaken through all the national registrations for the first quarter of 1902. Fortunately the name Josephine was rare for that period: the only match being on December 25th, 1901 for the birth of a

Josephine Churchill at 60 Langdon Road, Tufnel, in the district of Islington. This birth is almost certainly that of "our" Butler, the date corresponding to that given on her death certificate. Having been born with the name Churchill without, of course, any connection with that illustrious family, provided her with a passport to "fame" and entrance, no doubt, to social and influential circles. By claiming in Court that "her family had disowned her" she was attempting to reinforce the fictitious connection to the Churchills. However her wild claims at the Ambulance Station that she "had been brought up by the Churchill family" was truthful only by the fact that her father was Albert George Churchill, a laundryman, neither a builder as noted in court nor even an "Irish earl".

There is no Christian name for Butler's husband on the death certificate, a line being drawn through first name and occupation. No marriage was found in the registers but then she implied that this took place abroad. The Court reported that she had been cut off from her family when she married and that she was subsequently divorced before 1939. Although she penciled in a career for Mr Butler as a Secret Service colonel working undercover in France and dying of his wounds in 1947, according to the Court report he was an alcoholic.

Butler claims on the dustjacket of her book that from 1969 she undertook numerous lecture tours, "raising money for various charities and cancer research". (No evidence has been found in corroboration.) Having alleged that she had worked for the Theatre of Intelligence from 1942, she was able to rely upon her "detailed knowledge" of Enigma and Ultra and the work of Bletchley in the breaking of codes. However it is interesting to note that the librarian at Pickering, where she lived for many years, has no knowledge of such an eminent person.

Butler's death certificate states that she was a "Medical practitioner, retired". The Medical Registers carry no acknowledgement of such a person in any of her name combinations. Since specialism in the war was utilised, one cannot imagine that a qualified doctor would be permitted to remain at an ambulance station or work as a clerk. She was not addressed by this title in court. Her qualifications, as stated on the dustjacket of her book, were as impressive in the field of medicine as one has come to expect from her fertile imagination. She claims to have studied medicine and sociology at the Sorbonne where "she qualified as a surgeon", later assisting Marie Curie and Thierry de Martell in their cancer research until 1938. However she stated that she had never practised medicine in England: early retirement at thirty-six does seem premature, especially in wartime.

In 1991, Dr Josephine Butler published her second book of wartime exploits under the title *Cyanide in My Shoe* (This England Books, 1991), the title being the name given to Chapter 15 in her first book. In fact the full text of both books is almost identical in every respect except for the cover blurb, which explains that Dr Butler, a cancer specialist, has kept silent for 40 years (the previous book gave the years as 35) before revealing "her own extraordinary role in Europe's struggle for freedom". She includes photographs of Churchill and of a Lysander, besides, helpfully, a map of France showing her long walk during which she nearly took her cyanide pill because she was hungry and thirsty. The book was also produced in large print and talking book editions. As Nigel West comments "the fact that the author managed to publish the same book twice is itself testimony to her enterprise, if not to her imagination".

In 1944 her own counsel, Mr Sidney Isaacs, being aware no doubt of all the facts, used stronger language when summing up her personality in the hope of avoiding a custodial sentence for his client. He labelled her as "mentally unstable".

In her book, Butler stated that when she met Winston Churchill for a final visit, he instructed her to wait at least twenty years before writing the story of the Secret Circle. Remarking he would be dead by that time and unable to answer awkward questions, he warns her not to quote names or places that might be identified. She writes of her last interview with Winston Churchill, quoting his advice:

"He smiled at me. 'Others will undoubtedly write books. They will write fiction and non-fiction and near fiction — I ask only one thing, Jay Bee, let yours be truthful.'"

"I promised that, if ever I did write a book, I would write only the truth, and this I have done to the best of my ability. This is not a work of fiction or even near fiction. It is a true account of the years I spent as a member of the Secret Circle."

But there never was a Secret Circle . . . just as there never was a titled Lady Josephine Butler.

ISIS publish a wide range of books in large print, from fiction to biography. A full list of titles is available free of charge from the address below. Alternatively, contact your local library for details of their collection of ISIS large print books.

Details of ISIS complete and unabridged audio books are also available.

Any suggestions for books you would like to see in large print or audio are always welcome.

7 Centremead
Osney Mead
Oxford OX2 0ES
(01865) 250333